Leap: From Faith to Empowerment

By Katya Kathleen Williamson

ISBN 978-1-959457-02-2

Library of Congress Control Number: 2025926843

Published in the United States by

Blue Jay Ink

Dedication

To Joan Dudek, writer, daughter of irreplaceable Rachel, artist/musician:

Joan's parting words "hold on to your intentions" have kept me going throughout the years to complete this book.

There are tales of her riding her horse from the middle of orange groves past Riverside freeways, and often I feel as if I can still see her when I pass by the 14th Street exit on the 91. There she sits astride a golden horse, championing on women writers whose words have made a difference.

And
to "The Ocean of Love"

To The Reader

Even though the following stories are specific to my life, they are parables for yours. Use them as springboards, for they are *testaments that sources have already entered your life to be of service to you*, waiting to help you discover the meaning in your life that you have been searching for. Not only will these tales embellish your life, your life will benefit as mine has from:

Taking a LEAP of Faith.

Contents

Prologue

Little Legs at the Lincoln Memorial

I am five years old, standing with little legs on the white glistening marble floor of the Lincoln Memorial. Night lights shine on Lincoln's commanding presence in his giant chair, wide arms resting on its sides, staunch legs to the floor. A solemn gaze looks off to the far distance, and I am overwhelmed that he was the one who freed the slaves!

Walking to the memorial's edge, I stare out at the Washington Monument, another beacon in the darkness, banners of light sweeping over it. In the cool night air, the dark Reflecting Pool shimmers with ripples between the two. Surrounded by this grandeur and history of humanity, I am caught in a symmetry of light, symbolism and order.

Down the long Washington Mall I see the U.S. Capitol, this seat of government also infused in light, the statue of the Indian woman Sacajawea gazing from its top since the 1800's.

What is it that sweeps in from distant places reflecting humanitie's singular status on this planet? How is it that at any age, any place and time we can feel messages that come from ancient memories?

Moving from my five-year-old self to the present, this book of essays is in recognition of this precious legacy that we share in our web of connection with the universe and each other.

Introduction

"Action has Magic, Grace and Power in it.
Whatever you think you can do,
Or believe you can do, **Begin it.***"* *

"Why don't you write a book that will help others take 'Leaps of Faith' in their lives like you do? So they will also 'Go on Faith.' After all, you've been teaching this now for three decades; it could turn their lives around."

These words from friends and participants in countless worldwide women's writing retreats slipped off my back as I have known many other pioneering women who have taken risks in their lives as well.

But in the early 1990's a friend, Marilyn Sequoia, gave me a specially framed picture inscribed in her own calligraphy that read: "Katya Leads By Going" to commemorate our meeting in Yellowstone National Park where I was a writer-in-residence from 1991-1994. And sixteen years later, at a "Celebration Ceremony" in California when my book *Bringing the Soul Back Home: Writing in the New Consciousness* ("Compass Books", U.K.) was published, she presented me with this same image and message in a glossier frame and printed colored picture.

She did this at the exact moment when I began to recount how she had given me the other when I was speaking from a

stage honoring my life of empowering women and this publication of *Bringing the Soul Back Home.* There I had been
asked to tell the audience the story of my life and how I had
helped women empower themselves as a model that would
be used to honor other women in similar ceremonies for their
accomplishments.

In the picture, a blond woman points ahead at a curve
around a corner as she swiftly moves towards it. Why does
she so urgently need to get there? And where does it lead? She
is pulled by some larger force along with the other women
behind her, one silhouetted in blue with arm upraised seemingly shouting "Wait! Wait!" as the leader points *"This Way!"*
A third tries to catch up as she holds onto the dress of the one
in front of her, a briefcase in hand. "Don't leave me behind!"

Marilyn and I had met at another pivotal moment at the
debut of "Shards of Yellowstone," my first reading from the
book of poetry written as the writer in residence. Driving two
hours on dark roads from Lake to Madison Junction, she could
have collided with buffalo who frequented the unlit roads at
night in the Park. A poet herself, she was on sabbatical, and
it was another coincidence that we both lived close to each
other in California.

Then, in 2012, late one night in my own writing retreat in
Joshua Tree, California, a silver-haired woman exuding bright
energy and penetrating insight quizzed me about my life. In
front of a life-size portrait of Avatar Meher Baba whose eyes
seemed positively lit up, this coach/therapist caught hold of a

tail of a comet when she said with great emphasis:
>   *"You **must** write your stories down.*
>   *They are so unusual and will help many."*

Her name was also Marilyn (O'Connor) and her enthusiasm was so real I actually felt these stories wanting to come alive on the pages, imagining them helping others actualize their greatest dreams. Looking that night outside at the starry desert skies, the "astonishment" Marilyn conveyed for this writing was palpable.

The next morning at the writer's desk, I asked myself "what would I want to know from another woman's life experience that would help me towards greater self-realization? And I wrote these questions:

>   *"What lessons did the author learn about 'Taking a Leap*
>   *of Faith' against all obstacles?"*
>   *"What were her life experiences that I could apply to my*
>   *own life?"*
>   *"How did she actually do this?" and "What did it feel like?"*
>   *"And, finally how did she believe enough in the Unknown,*
>   *that she could surrender to it enough for her to allow it to*
>   *take her where she needed to go?"*

Especially in those late night hours in moments when we've all had the urgency to understand the meaning of our lives, I've dug deep into my own journey of self-discovery, and have:

1. *"Gone on Faith by instinct"*
2. *"Held the rope, knowing it was leading somewhere"*
3. *"Held this rope for my own arts and writing projects over forty years that have helped other individuals and larger arts communities"*
4. *"Learned to listen **deeply** as a leader in support groups for women artists to foster the emergence of their own creativity."*
5. *"Believed in a deeper part of my being in the signs and synchronicities that happen in all of our lives over and over again if we can acknowledge them."*

In short, my life has focused on "*Listening,*" as these words by author Phyllis Theroux (which were coincidentally on the last piece of scrap paper picked off the floor in a recent move) conveyed:

> *"I was sitting quietly in my own despair when I heard a voice. It wasn't my voice. It wasn't anybody else's voice either. But it came from such a deep and Delphic place within my being that I did not question its authority."*
> *"I have acquired the habit of listening—the way a servant listens for the sound of the bell—*
> *as if my life depended upon it."*

Whether it is about hearing how to live one's life or listening for the writing or creativity to come, this listening has always guided me on. Discovering that piece of paper on the floor reconfirmed what is most important: that we are gently companioned throughout our lives with guides and muses waiting to assist us to do the soul work of our lives.

Even though the following stories are specific to my life, they are parables for yours. Use them as springboards, for they are *testaments that sources have already entered your life to be of service to you*, waiting to help you discover the meaning in your life that you have been searching for. Not only will these tales embellish your life, your life will benefit as mine has from:

Taking a LEAP of Faith.

— *1* —

The First Vision

The ice was encrusted on the sidewalks of Santa Fe on the eve of a New Year. It reflected my agitated mood as I walked back and forth from the Inn of La Posada to the center of town. Ending my long-term career in arts administration to become a full-fledged writer, I felt as cold as the elaborate ice sculptures in the inn's courtyard.

Earlier that month, I had witnessed the first of two full moons that would rise the last month of 1990. Its oval presence flooded a hilltop home in Los Angeles and I knew it signaled big change. That night I had already made reservations with a friend to go to Santa Fe to celebrate the season, see the ferolitas (glowing candles in brown paper bags of sand) traditionally lining government and town buildings, and visit Chimayo, the healing chapel Lourdes of the Southwest. Come hell or high water, I was bound for Santa Fe.

But in between then and the trip, fate had released me more quickly than planned from my administrative duties, and now, in contrast to this earlier brightness, I was in the throes of uncertainty. I did find solace when we moved to the dowager hotel of Santa Fe, the La Fonda, that had long corridors that reminded me of ones I'd wandered on transatlantic ocean liners as a child. Walking through them over and over again, they calmed me as I paced back and forth feeling a stranger in a strange world.

Then one early morning, the churning in my mind made it difficult to sleep and with the moon outside sliding towards fullness, I drew a bath in an antique tub. As I took my first step in the water, a surprising surge of insight swept through me, and I suddenly knew how, as I was at the edge of profound changes in my life, so too were scores of women. That it was rushing towards all of us like some fast-moving train was a given, and I knew, in all certainty, how dramatic this transformation would be.

There had been other moments of insight in my life, but I had never experienced anything like this before. Dazed by what had just happened, I got out of the tub, and picked up my journal to record how, as I was poised to take this leap into the unknown, there was a similar evolutionary leap about to happen to all women everywhere.

Returning to LA in time for the arrival of the New Year, and the next full moon, I was joined by three women artists for dinner where the conversation dwelled upon how this "once in a blue moon" month was a time of expanded female power, and how after years of advancement, there were still so many obstacles to full empowerment.

"You've gone a long way, baby" wasn't far enough. It was now: "And you are supposed to go much further...the global society depends upon you to bring a new balance into the world...

if you will but *listen*. This is the time, this is the Awakening."
Our conversation underscored the need to communicate this.

Then, at the New Year's Eve celebration the next evening
in Malibu, I wandered out a few minutes before midnight onto
a large balcony with a 360-degree view of the Pacific Ocean,
Channel Islands and Bony Mountain Ridge. Suspended above
the ocean, I was just in time for this second full moon to make
its stunning entrance over the ridge of the mountain to my
left, its edges embracing the light as the moon behind it grew
larger and larger.

Watching it grow, I began to realize how the chain of
events in this "blue moon" month and the second full moon
were the actual harbingers of this new age for women. Its
glimmering radiance was the visual symbol of this shift in
consciousness that was beginning to happen around the globe,
and I knew then this shift into our new global status must be
communicated and encouraged.

Now thirty years later, I have worked with countless
women around the world to honor their authentic selves and
speak their truth through writing in classes, retreats, workshops, and sacred site tours.

And it was the month of the two blue moons, the vision
in the bathtub, and the second full moon rising over Malibu
that signaled this momentous beginning.

———— ➤ *2* ◀———— ————

My Imagination

*"Don't Ever Forget to Believe in What **You Can't See:**
That's Imagination."*
*Spoken by actor Morgan Freeman portraying a famous author in
the film "The Miracle of Belle Isle"*

Climbing down from a large tree of corrugated bark at the Navy Line School beside the illustrious Hotel Del Monte in Monterey, California, I encountered my first lesson in speaking my truth. I was age seven. It was the 1950's, the hotel had been converted for administrative use by the Navy into an "Officer's Line School," a place where officers learned the rules of behavior and etiquette required to get ahead or lose their careers.

The tree was a meeting ground for the tribe of children of these men, and on that day, I met one of their fathers as I swung onto the ground. Engaging him in a story I was particularly proud of, I most likely went way over the top into the fantasy world, because at the end of my tale, he said those pivotal words: *"What an imagination you have."*

But it wasn't a compliment. His tone somehow conveyed that this imagination didn't fit prescribed standards of society, and unaware of how my words might disturb a rules-oriented military man, I knew something was wrong.

On a daily basis, our rebellious tribe of children ran around the hotel's grounds that housed three swimming pools and large grassy areas. In the enclosed area there were quarters, offices in the hotel, movie theaters, and acres of hills that was our own prescribed playground.

The daily game at five p.m. was to flee inside the hotel when Taps started on the dot and the American flag was removed from the flag pole. Everything came to a halt. If you were outside, you had to stop whatever you were doing and stand still, and if you were in a car, especially in uniform, you had to get out of the car and salute the flag. Needless to say, there were collisions between the adults living up to rigid codes of performance and free-wheeling children.

The officer's tone with the words "what an *imagination* you have" somehow has stayed with me through the years to return unexpectedly, especially when embarking upon a new creative project or choosing a potentially risky fork in the road.

Use of the imagination has brought about so many positive solutions for society and ushered in many new frontiers, but it is still met with widespread skepticism. Why does that persist, especially after Einstein's enduring statement: "The Imagination is more important than Knowledge"? Hugely enlivening to the aspirations and creativity of all, many must still wade through these misapprehensions to chart their own course.

For example, in the movie *Never Land*, Scottish playwright

E.M. Barrie, the creator of Peter Pan that has enthralled countless audiences over time, is portrayed by his high society patrons as bordering on too fantastical. Even when most of his plays were successful, when one was a potential failure these patrons were ready to crucify him. Then came Peter Pan.

What child hasn't been completely taken over by the pure desire for flying, and Peter Pan brought this instinctive urge in all audiences to moments of rapture. When a new project was just birthing and he began creating the plot of the story, the movie showed how the muse enabled him to see shafts of golden light around potential characters. When he met four boys in a city park who became models for the key characters in the Peter Pan story as pirates, Indians, and the famous "lost boys," and became their guardian after their mother dies, they regained their faith in life through his help by his rekindling their imagination.

For most children at that early age, the belief that one could fly like Peter Pan, Wendy, or Tinkerbell, has been so rich and free that they have seen no separation from themselves and that reality. What happens to that vital source of energy at other times in our lives? How do we lose the *wonder* that is our birthright, especially when we become adults?

Whether or not this actually happened at the debut of the first performance of Peter Pan in the late 1800's in Scotland, the movie depicts the laughter of children from a nearby orphanage Barrie purposely brought into the theatre to be present on opening night. Their joy was so palpable that the older adults soon lost their brittle self-consciousness and began to relax and laugh with them. Seeing the play through their innocent eyes, the older patrons became free enough to return home to their true selves and to accept their own inalienable innocence.

Like my flying down that tree to a disdainful reaction, the movie reminded me that when judgment from an internal or external source occurs, ***that*** is the time to move forward into authentic action.

Remaining courageous in the face of the critic is tantamount to birthing new life. What a privilege it has been in my work to witness peoples' eyes light up over and over again when they have realized the unique and innate source of creativity that dwells within them and they can utilize it to convey their own truth and presence in the world.

"If You Have Faith, You Can Fly."
E.M. Barrie

French Toast

French toast, or rather pieces of dried toast with cinnamon mixed with sugar was a sibling treat our first days in a foreign country as we tried to cope with why we were there. The cinnamon was poured onto this buttered toast after it had been vigorously mixed with white sugar and was a constant at any time of day or night, the comfort we knew somehow to create, a ritual we could live by.

I am reminded of it as I sit years later eating "whirled cinnamon toast" from Trader Joes, a faint but indissoluble memory. "Why does it still come up?" My red-headed sister was wearing a French beret with green and red designs on it, probably trying to feel more at home, as she doled out the toast, her twin brother lapping it up as I continued to mix more and more white sugar with cinnamon to keep the toast coming.

We were five then when we landed in France, unexpectedly ushered there by quickly changing Navy orders—two parents, three kids, our little brother not yet born. They were fourteen, I was nine and we had just been wrestled away from Paradise Hawaii, warm and sunny. Here it was gloomy, rainy and cold when we arrived at the end of November.

The large black furnace downstairs in the basement

constantly needed to be re-lit in this drafty three story ornate French house, and who could believe there was one bathtub on clawed feet with only enough water each night for us all to take a bath? The last person always dipped into grey slimy cold water. I remember my Dad going up and down those basement stairs to re-stoke the furnace at all hours.

Looking back, or course, it was a special opportunity to view a whole different world that would always push me further in later years to travel as an obsession. It did expand my consciousness in ways I could never have fathomed. But since we'd had to unexpectedly vacate our existence on Oahu in Pearl Harbor, the ill-fated Arizona nearby, and leave school in the middle of the year, I was heart broken. I loved playing the piano with an eye on the future as a pianist and mixing with all sorts Asian and Hawaiian populations who felt like family.

Driving 5000 miles across country was an adventure in its own way. School books on my lap as my mother attempted to keep up my fourth grade learning, while watching the changes in this vast country go by were more than memorable. Exploring New York City for the first time and then boarding the huge ocean liner, the S.S. United States, at its port were all one of a kind unique lifetime events.

The second day we arrived in Le Vesinet, a French suburb outside Paris, we were herded onto turtle-like shellacked Army buses to the American school in Garche, and I began to understand how I'd always be part of a tribe of military kids who were in the same situation. They held out their hands in welcome, implying you "do have a home with us if nowhere else," a floating non-home that would predict my life of travel and need for community for decades.

It didn't help that our parents continued their feud over power, so the home environment was anything but peaceful. True, they were coping as best as they could to Dad's unexpected change in orders where he would be the first from his class at Annapolis to have his own Carrier. But that changed abruptly, and as he had already given notice as Chief of Staff, we had to go!! He'd thrived in that position, as I had in Hawaii, and I always felt that Paris was the beginning in earnest of the downhill slide of the family.

"Well, kids," they asked as they sat us down on the couch in a row together, "We can go to Brazil, the California desert, or France. What would you like to do?" We looked vacantly at each other, and the determining factor was that my older brother had taken French, so it was decided: "France!"

Years later, I can understand why Isabel Allende said if she hadn't been deported to Venezuela from Chile after its coup, she'd never have become a writer. Being in exile helped determine this path when she was forced to re-create in words depicting where she was and where she came from. I was younger than she, but as an Outsider also at ten my psyche knew to become a writer, not understanding but knowing it was my one saving grace to comprehend this series of life events and there would be many more in the future that my writing would help me understand as well.

Thus, the act of writing became my stability and clarity that has sustained me throughout my life.

But right then, we didn't understand why French people were throwing eggs at our Buick or we why we were in this drafty mansion on 7 Rue Alphonse Pallu inhabited by ghosts. Or why the atmosphere felt so stormy, the Algerian War soon to take to the streets of Paris.

Life went on. Dad was assigned to the Ecole Militaire at NATO (the institution for military officers Napoleon started) that was located just across the long grassy expanse to the Eiffel Tower. A vivid memory is our arrival on Thanksgiving Day standing as a family on the white marble bridge at the Palais de Chaillot over the Seine staring across to that extraordinary view of the Eiffel Tower.

In the beginning, there were special times as a family, whirling in our tiny new French Simca around the Arc de Triumph not knowing where to go, or when we got lost in the Louvre, the only way we came eye to eye with the famous Mona Lisa. The Egyptian statuary from the Rameses period also opened a world of significance for me and later pushed me into a career in Art History.

Like those who freeze initially in similar circumstances, my siblings and I finally started to adjust better to this new culture. But then, everything changed again. We were to return to the States in just two years to a new post in Washington, D.C. after our little brother was born and medical conditions were supposedly better for him in the States. I remember watching the tiny yellow bassinet that held him, our three and a half month old brother, taken across the waters on a boat by some stranger. For some reason we were in another craft to get to the SS Independence leaving from Cannes, and I remember yelling, "Take care of our little brother! He's part of this family too!"

It has been said, "Forgiveness is about Letting Go of All Hope For a Better Past." What to forgive? The circumstances, the military system, chaotic times, needing to adjust to different cultures?

Through its continual wrestling of words, writing has the capacity to eke clarity in chaos and confusion, to bring about healing. And then there is always French Toast!

4

The Feminine Mystique

"The Problem that has No Name — simply the fact that American women are kept from growing to their full human capacities is taking a far greater toll on the physical and mental health of our country than any known disease."

Betty Friedan, The Feminine Mystique, 1963

"What is the meaning of life?" At fifteen, I sat bolt upright on black wrought iron steps behind a new brick house in Alexandria, Virginia. Staring at a glimpse of the Potomac River through sparse landscape where trees had recently been cut down for suburbs outside Washington, D.C., this sudden question floored me. Then it was followed by "why are we here?"

Returning from France in a Navy family in the early 1960's, relieved to no longer be an outsider in a foreign country, I sensed yet another kind of isolation. Out in those suburbs there was an overall alienation of the housewives to their lot in life. Silent screams were put under the carpet every morning as my mother and her counterparts chaffed at being put out to pasture while the men, CEO's of corporations, military and

Foreign Service officers, were entitled to follow their individual identities in the workforce.

"Ask not what you can do for yourself, but what you can do for your country!" On the other hand, on a life-changing walk a year before up another Virginia hillside, I had the excited reaction as a young teenager to JFK's groundbreaking quote. Vivid in the winter bleakness, it pinpointed a destiny for women of my generation that would be markedly different from the past.

Pacing quickly up and down the hill to absorb these riveting words, I looked forward to fulfilling this "light bearer's" prediction as a groundbreaker for women's roles in society. I had intuited this "call," but it was sooner than expected! I still had a few years to grow up.

Meanwhile, mothers seemed frozen in their roles, obsolescent in their own time. Co-opted by the patriarchy to postpone their professional/ personal actualization to return America to normalcy after World War II, they had been pressured by media and magazines run by men to tend to their 2.5 children in "Leave it to Beaver" families. They "should" be happy as immaculate housewives and mothers in blissful domesticity, and I vowed I would not be caught like Lot's Wife turned into a pillar of salt to become a Stepford wife.

On those back steps near Mount Vernon, the plantation of the Father of our Country, I wondered how the Declaration of Independence could declare all individuals "to be considered equal" but had not lived up to that promise for women.

Years later, another life-changing experience similar to

those on the hillside and back porch propelled my life forward. Enrolled at Western College for Women in Oxford,
Ohio that was started as the "western" Mount Holyoke by the
founders of the first emancipated women's college in 1835,
I was impressed with its commitment to social justice and
advancement of women. Two months before arriving as a
freshman, it was the training site in the summer of 1964 for
the famous Freedom Riders before they left for Mississippi
to help Southern Blacks gain voting rights.

Even after they had been informed of the three men mur-
dered in Mississippi who had been leading in these efforts for
that vote, they still continued on to the state.

In my case, however, even though I had planned an even-
tual career in international relations bolstered by access to the
ten percent of the college's five hundred women being from
foreign countries, it felt too far from the stimulation of the East
Coast for me, and one day in the middle of the second semes-
ter I bolted! Walking to the end of its cobblestone entryway of
stone walls and elaborate pedestals of lights on both sides, I
boarded a Greyhound bus for Philadelphia to visit a friend at
the University of Pennsylvania before returning to Virginia.

Little did I know as I fled on the Greyhound that I was in
for a major life change, for in my hands was the groundbreaking book by Betty Friedan, *The Feminine Mystique*, published
two years before. Reading it from cover-to-cover during the
ride from Oxford to Philadelphia, I emerged from the bus a
totally new woman.

The trumpet had sounded! Demonstrating how her fellow alumni from Smith College in the late 1950's, among the most entitled and intelligent women of the time, were still dependent upon the dictates of men and society for their sense of self and identity, her interviews showed that 89% of them had discarded their education to get married and have children, letting go expectations for their careers and the advancement of their individual identities. The impetus my generation would use to begin sorely needed breakthroughs in women's empowerment, the book was a clarion call for advancement.

Challenging the myth that all women in previous generations and in the 1950's and 60's were happy in their roles as homemakers, it chillingly pronounced that "the Feminine Mystique had succeeded in burying millions of American women alive." It lit a firestorm of awareness that created the Women's Movement of the 1960's and 1970's, and launched N.O.W., the National Organization of Women with Friedan as its first President. Spurring on Consciousness Raising groups in the sixties and seventies, there was a landslide of new consciousness in women. Groups turned therapeutic sessions into political action as it was revolutionary for women to speak to each other about topics that were previously taboo: husbands, dating, economic dependence, children and abortion, loneliness, and isolation.

With each member allowed to speak without interruption, additional trust and solidarity was built in non-hierarchical formats. Sociologist Carol Hanisch's ground-breaking article of the time, "The Personal is Political" clarified that because discrimination had been so pervasive, subtly deadening and oppressive, CR groups also enabled women to verbalize feelings they might have never realized they had before.

My life-changing bus ride from Ohio to Philadelphia vindicating my initial teenage intuition and the continued historical influence of the Women's Consciousness groups is still alive in the contemporary women's retreats and workshops I have facilitated in writing in the last three decades. But even today when women arrive at them, it is clear that self-esteem is still a major issue and these supportive writing experiences have helped self-confidence and assertion to prosper.

If I hadn't boarded that bus, and taken the journey from a college founded by Mary Lyon, the first advocate of education for *all* women, not just the privileged few, I wouldn't have understood the urgency in 1965 that is still even more so in 2025 for women to come forward. Their skills, ingenuity and intelligence are even more necessary today in stabilizing our individual, human and global condition.

———————— ► 5 ◄ ————————

Eulogy JFK, EMVEEHI

Mount Vernon High December, 1963

Eulogy written as Editor of this high school newspaper, Alexandria, Virginia (A Scholastic award-winning paper honored by the Scholastic press of Columbia University, NYC) Upon the Death of President John F. Kennedy

"We are young as he was young. And in his death, we, as the Nation's youth, have lost as much or more as any group or individual. For to us he was the embodiment of our young hopes and aspirations. Although we have lost the man, let us not now lose his spirit—the youthful, hopeful qualities which made him one with us and humanity. As he was torn from life before the fruition of his goals, let us continue to prepare, as he was prepared, so that we might some-day achieve those goals. And if someday we too are destroyed, let it be said: "this

Youth had such promise, the enduring quality of what they could have achieved will not perish with them." "*It is rather for us to be here dedicated to the great task remaining before us— that from this honored dead we take increased devotion to that cause for which he gave his last full measure of devotion; that we here highly resolve that he shall not have died in vain." (paraphrased from the 'Gettysburg Address')*

6

The Pilgrimage Home

*"Humans, even nomadic ones, need a sense of home.
Home need not be one place or any place at all, but
every home has two essential elements: a sense of
community and, even more important, a history."*
From BLISS, by Eric Weiner

I found home when I was just twenty years old in Boston. It was then I saw Meher Baba's portrait—unknowingly—for the first time.

Following a boyfriend from the Department of State in Washington, D.C. in 1967 to live in Boston, I spent hours in Cambridge Square writing about "where was home?" Crisscrossing the globe as a child, I was living out the intriguing and sometimes unsettling pattern of exploring new geographies and cultures to assess where I belonged. It was the era when coffee houses thrived and music poured out on the streets from every corner: Maria Muldar's "Midnight at the Oasis" exuding from one cafe while the Kingston Trio "riding through the streets of Boston, never to return," came from another.

Then one day, as I stepped over ice and snow on the threshold of an apartment between Harvard and M.I.T. on

Commonwealth Avenue, I passed the portrait of Meher Baba on an altar that would eventually launch a firestorm in my life

Who was he, this man with dark hair, oval face, penetrating black eyes, and a large mustache? Taking one glimpse, I passed quickly by, it never occurring to me that I might have met my destiny. Dressed in white, a garland of blossoms around his neck, with a compassionate smile, his famous quote of *"Don't Worry, Be Happy"* shortened from *"Do your best, and then Don't Worry, Be Happy, and I will do the rest"* was below the picture. Then it was two years before he "dropped his body," at a time when he supposedly cast a last net over those connected to him.

In contrast to the brittle cold outside, this was the beginning of a tremendous spiritual awakening but it was not until thirty-eight years later it would come to light in Glastonbury, England. A special person named Patricia would introduce me to him, explaining that "bringing awareness to our spiritual condition in the West" was his ultimate goal.

At a friend's birthday party in August, 2005 a group of illustrious Glastonians gathered in a lush English garden where I relaxed after leading a strenuous tour for women artists. Leaving the garden to move back into the living room I was suddenly stunned by an amazing sight.

As if he had just come out of a remote cave after years of meditation, an ancient sage with silver hair had entered the room. In an Indian Sadhu outfit, long white shirt over pants, his face accentuated by a small goatee, he emanated centuries of wisdom. But in reality, it was actually Patricia, who I was still to meet, who would become my mentor for Meher Baba.

She had arrived wearing a white blouse with a scalloped top and flowered skirt, an attractive silver belt at her waist. As this unexplainable double vision of a Sadhu overlapping her being was beyond anything I could have possibly imagined, my mind blanked out. Turning abruptly away, I spun back into the festivities in the garden and took in a breath of fresh air. But in that instant a signal had been made. How could I have known my life would be changed in such a dramatic fashion? Like the first glimpse of Meher Baba in Boston, I didn't put another thought to it, but with Patricia's face and outfit shape-shifting in that way, I had been put on notice that the "invisible" world would soon become an indelible part of my reality.

At an afternoon tea a week after the birthday in the same living room where the sage appeared, Patricia gently described Meher Baba, recounting her monumental experiences of how he had come to her. That was when I said, quite innocently, "Now I *do* remember seeing a picture of him years before in 1967 in an apartment in Cambridge, Massachusetts," not realizing this would mark the beginning of my extraordinary journey with him.

That was when she invited me to a gathering she would host a week later at her home to do watercolor painting on silk, make flower essences in her garden, and eat a delicious meal. Perhaps intuiting a sea change in my life, I was strangely resistant, and late Friday night before that Saturday called to say I couldn't make it. "You have to come," she said, "Your place has already been arranged."

After a difficult summer, meeting her and an offer to be at a friend's home that overlooked the prominent St. John's Cathedral until Christmas, my body began to relax. Feeling a bit like the proverbial phoenix rising from the ashes, I had a stunning dream of St. Francis on my first night there where I had lost everything, moved through a door to the unknown and then recovered into a new world. I had been readied for this next chapter with Patricia and Meher Baba.

That Saturday morning my feet felt like lead as I climbed two steep hills, but when I arrived, the group was in the back garden effusive with flowers and lush apple orchards, the small city of Wells and its Cathedral a stunning view in the far distance. Everyone was in high spirits in the bright sunshine as we proceeded to make flower essences there.

"Come with me into the sanctuary," Patricia announced after a sumptuous lunch. "Meher Baba would like each of you to receive a gift from him." Deciding this would not influence me in the least, I walked into an ambiance of soft pink peace. She turned to me and said, "Baba would like to give you the largest bouquet of roses you will ever receive."

I was immediately swept away by tears filling my eyes and chills going through my body. Nine months before, at the end of a reading with a spiritual intuitive in Glastonbury, I had been told: "Whenever you see a rose, know that those who love you from the other side are sending you their love, are with you, and you will never feel alone." Baba was handing me the largest bouquet of roses I was ever to receive! How did he know? *That was it: He Just Knew. He always knew.*

Minutes before we sat down in the sanctuary, Patricia had also shown us flower essences taken from plants and trees at Meher Baba's retreat in Meherabad, India southeast of Mumbai. One of them had been made from the banyan tree, symbolized as "The Tree of Worldly and Universal knowledge." I had connected to a banyan tree that was my makeshift home as a child on O'ahu, Hawaii, so those words about the tree created another knowing through my body. Resistance was beginning to melt, and it was as if the whole day started to dissolve my strong hesitation towards a sudden connection to the Divine. Was this calling linking me to Baba that began with that first sighting of his picture in 1967? And was that because, as it had been implied by Patricia, that I might have been with him in other lifetimes? It was a great puzzle.

"I already have a spiritual guide, Paramahansa Yogananda," I thought, with whom I had found comfort for twenty years at the Lake Shrine in Los Angeles. "Why do I need another one?" Nothing made sense in reaction to this large-scale shift of consciousness that the logical mind couldn't explain. But in the weeks following, Patricia invited me to come again to the sanctuary. "Baba wanted to tell me something of my his-tory—was I interested?" Of course I was curious.

Through her, he explained that I'd been a monk in many lifetimes, and, in one particular one, had been a Tibetan where

I demonstrated a remarkable devotion to God. Even though I was now living in a vastly different time and culture, that devotion was apparently influencing the fate of my life. Not even sure about the concept of reincarnation, with nothing making sense, there was something about what he said that did. In fact, everything he relayed through Patricia felt instinctively "right" to me. Because of this, I was more and more drawn to our connection.

I was also influenced by Patricia's extraordinary story about how Meher Baba became a pivotal part of her life and all these events began to make a deep impression on me:

Once a Midlands school teacher in England, now with a family of two grown children and grandchildren, she had moved with her engineer husband to start a B & B in Glastonbury to develop her spirituality. In the 1990's in Cornwall, she had been told in a dream by an invisible presence in white that she should read an article in the newspaper the following morning on Kashmir. She promptly forgot this. But upon awakening, as she turned to two full pages on the war-torn area that described its ongoing territorial conflict between Pakistan and India, she took notice. In the dream she been told she was to travel there, that seemed an impossible journey.

No travel agents would give insurance to Westerners to go there, and she had never traveled alone without her husband, especially in such dangerous conditions. But somehow when a last agent finally acquiesced, she knew she must go. She still didn't know who this invisible being was who had arrived that night in her dream, but soon two guests arrived at her door of the B & B carrying a book with Meher Baba's picture on the cover. Then she knew it was him!

Now driving in Kashmir with a young frightened driver above hilly mountain terrain, they were stopped at the border by an agitated guard brandishing a gun. Demanding they get out the car, they stood frozen for several moments until, to their relief, the guard's superior arrived who greatly admonished him and waved them on. Finally in safety at a houseboat, alone because of the Civil War, she received special attention for all her needs and received first-hand his teachings when his presence came to her.

His million plus followers around the world know him as the "Avatar for All Ages" — "*coming not to teach, but to awaken,*" incarnating before as Buddha, Jesus, Ram, Mohammed and other sages. But as "no one listened" before, he made a commitment to take an oath of silence, and from his early twenties, he never spoke again, a great sacrifice for one known to have a beautiful singing and speaking voice.

After Patricia received his teachings in Kashmir, she then began to guide me and a group of both English and Americans about his teachings. However, still cautious about anything "that didn't make sense," it took me a long time to make a connection.

When the wave of religious sages arrived from the East in the 1960's to infuse United States culture with different perceptions of faith, it was confusing who might be the right one to learn from, if at all. As if looking for water in the desert, I had been on my own quest upon arrival in California in the early 1980's to find a spiritual teacher who would speak authentically to me.

I had to laugh when I spoke of Meher Baba, and friends said, "You mean, Sai Baba, the one with the hair?" ("No, as a matter of fact, not"). That's how Westerners, especially from the U.S. still differentiated between the complexities of the masters from India and elsewhere, so many, as they were quick to point out, who were called "Baba" (meaning "father" in many languages).

In 1982, I discovered Paramahansa Yogananda, a great influence in the West especially in California and Arizona where he created a number of temples. Instructed by his master Sri Yukteswar to leave India to bring Kriya Yoga to the West in the 1920's, he knew not a word of English but became fluent overnight when asked to lecture on the boat bringing him to America, and was quickly accepted by spiritual peoples in this country. That first day I walked into the Lake Shrine into its Court of All Religions where signs said "we are all one," I found a home base from 1984 to this defining moment in Glastonbury in 2005.

When Meher Baba claimed in our sessions that with many others I would help people to "awaken" to their spirituality, it felt strangely accurate. In the last three decades I have facil-itated many to discover and celebrate their innate creativity and awaken to themselves.

"*You Are Not Who You Think You Are*," Baba has said. "*You are much greater than you know*." His statement is for every living person on this planet, most unaware of their tremendous potential. Through him, it has been life changing to know we are part of a much larger scope of the Universe than we can possibly imagine, conscious of a small fraction of our place in it.

Many times in my life I have felt as if, to test my faith, I have been put in a lifeboat to bail out the water. I had to **See** things to **Believe Them**, which Baba knew, because on that summer day in August, 2005, I saw one reality juxtaposing another in Glastonbury, England, and he knew that was the only way I could accept that there are other realities to experience in this lifetime along with his immense presence in this world.

"To row back up the river is to try to exempt oneself
From being acted upon by the forces
that so urgently carry us all, **not toward safety**
but most surely toward salvation."

Kimberly C. Patton, a Harvard Divinity Chaplain

--- 7 ---

Beads in the Snow:
Our legacy from the 1960's

The poetic prelude to the creation of Artworks Gallery
in Hartford, Connecticut

In the Red Rock country of Colorado, copper red buttes
emerging out of white snow, I drove with a friend to a
long-established commune where people awaited us. But
now the roads had ended in the wilderness and our car
began rolling over mesa after mesa without a map to find
our destination. Lost even from where we left the road
behind, it was a miracle when the commune's trucks came
over the hill like a posse search party to find us. But then
when we got out of the car to greet those saviors, huge
amounts of beads fell in the snow from my friend's jewel-
ry-making kit. Like the colors of a life, beaded on a string,
I've always remembered them as portrayals of the nomadic
adventures of our generation in the 1960's and 1970's as
we hunted new meaning for existence with a unique sense
of freedom and excitement, and sometimes naivety.

Meeting life as a traveler, taking off on a Jack Kerouac

Journey "On the Road"

Trying to stowaway on board a steamer to New Zealand in San Francisco.

Looking at the heights and precipices of Big Sur over the ocean while hitchhiking back down the coast from San Francisco to LA to end the summer there.

"Tuesday Afternoon, I'm just beginning to see," hearing these words in a Moody Blues song near Zuma Beach, Malibu and in that one moment knowing I'd return to make California my home.

Kayaking on a cross country trip in all kinds of water, lakes, rivers, streams at national parks, in wilderness areas, and even on the San Francisco Bay, as we travelled from East to West on the northern route across the country to British Columbia.

Reaching deep into muddy waters to pull up a rarely seen giant Horseshoe Clam on Summer Solstice, eating marigolds, pounding fresh abalone for meals, sawing wood and building houses.

Walking through the woods and pulling pristine water from the well.

Lying under starry skies, stars reaching down to fuse with Indian energy that reached up to meet them late at night on land not inhabited since the Indians lived there decades before.

Building another house, a bear arriving in the orchard with three small children in the vicinity; what to do? British Columbia.

A honeymoon-like summer on an introductory trip of the Southwest: Floating in deep hot pools in the Sand Dunes Monument, Colorado; musicians' recitals in Ski Valley high above Taos, New Mexico; savoring Indians' wares at the Governor's Palace, Santa Fe, Aspen, Colorado; photographs above the giant Salt Lake in Salt Lake City, Utah .

Hot pools at Jemez Pueblo in the falling snow in January

Views of mountain peaks and herds of reindeer/ elk in near dark from the window while traveling on the cross-country train from Vancouver, Canada through the Rockies to Montreal to return east to a new life in Connecticut.

The moment on top of the Sandia Mountains, a blond woman with a giant snake wrapped around her being photographed, lights glinting below of Albuquerque, New Mexico

At Indian dances near the sacred Black Mesa; bright Hollyhocks in Santa Fe near the smallest and oldest church there; Chimayo, Lourdes of the Southwest with healing dirt in center hole in the sanctuary; Ghost Ranch, Abiquiu, New Mexico.

Beads in the Snow, like many of us of that generation, brightly colored beads, reds, greens, purples, blues, turquoise, pink, mauves, against the white snow: the blank canvas of revised expectations, a new society trying to find itself, some out there in the Red Rock country of Colorado, copper red buttes pushing their heads out of the white wilderness, others going back into the cities to bring revolutionary forms of productivity and new ways of working together, envisioning community in a world ready for social and cultural change.

————— *8* —————

The Artists' Cooperative Comes to Connecticut

It has been said that moving is one of the most difficult transitions one can have in life, after death and divorce. But in 1971, still a young adult, I took the chance opportunity to move to Connecticut to start a new life that would eventually impact the rest of it professionally and personally. With an illustrious photographer, we started a life together as a couple, but compared to where I'd lived in California and Washington, D.C., the colder darker climate in more conservative New England was hard to adjust to in those first years. However, luckily the warmth and connection of friends helped, many of whom Siegfried Halus had already made as a charismatic university professor. "Once a friend, always a friend" they say about New Englanders.

That was also the time to find an identity in the workplace, and the allure of Isamu Noguchi sculptures in the park setting of CIGNA Insurance Company's home office drew me for this first one as its newsletter editor. As an editor of a high school newspaper, I had the credentials to create the company's bi-weekly periodical while continuing to do my own writing at lunchtime on its spacious grounds.

But the day that Bill Doty died was a major wake up call to corporate consciousness. Tall, with listless blond hair over a pale face, this Manager of Publications and family man who'd worked for decades at this one job had kindly shown me the ropes of our small department in my first days. But one morning he'd left the building for his weekly trip to a subsidiary in Hartford. Upon arrival, he'd had a heart attack right at its entryway. I couldn't believe that the taciturn Vice President who informed us later that afternoon didn't speak of his contribution to the company or his unique personhood. Even the funeral afterward was lackluster at best, not giving him his due.

Shocked, I began riding up and down the company's silver escalators in its multi-tiered glass-filled enclosure, aimlessly contemplating what I was doing in this soulless place. The empty glass reflections outside seemed to mirror my distress, and I wondered if I'd ever feel at home in this iron-clad Northern environment.

It wasn't until I took a position at the Connecticut Commission on the Arts years later in the camaraderie of public arts and arts administrators, writers and artists that the light came through. In this post-Kennedy era when the arts were still nationally acknowledged as significant and essential for the country's identity, it was stimulating to go as a group from the Commission to see Alexander Calder unveil his famed Stegosaurus sculpture in front of a city building.

Watching him speak about his work after his almost fatal heart attack, I felt the poignancy witnessing these last years of this huge arts giant, knowing the transience of life compared to the art that would remain there.

This exciting time of integrating Hartford's unique history with the contemporary arts was also obvious at another installation where our group gathered again to watch the unveiling of a sculpture by Carl Andre, a nationally known artist. Installed in a park near the oldest museum in the country, the Wadsworth Atheneum, it was within walking distance from the infamous Charter Oak Tree where rebels hid the Constitution during the Revolutionary War.

And then, there was Evelyn Smith, Public Arts Coordinator. With easy assurance, she spearheaded a new arts movement for Connecticut artists through the symposium she organized called "Artists: How Do We Survive?" It was the first inkling of the work I would be immersed in for the next two decades, helping large numbers of artists locate opportunities that also demonstrated their contribution to society. As a special mentor, she confided that funds were soon coming from the federal government for those who would create community arts organizations to help artists, alerting me to this potential for fostering the arts. For this and the other seeds she planted for burgeoning arts endeavors she will always be remembered as she passed away too early.

With Evelyn's prediction and new confidence that money was coming through, I started preparation for founding a community arts organization that would eventually last in Hartford for thirty-two years. In its first moments as I birthed this vision, I was thrilled to hold the reins to make it realized, preparing numerous lists of the multitudinous tasks to be accomplished. For the first time in my life it felt like an extraordinary opportunity to utilize abilities that had never been tested before and it helped that I had met many artists in the city and outlying areas since I'd arrived and had an art history background. I could now see how an arts organization could serve their careers.

As I set out to locate key resources to make this a reality, it became concrete when I was offered office space and secretarial help by Reverend Ken South, Director, Hill Center, a community-based organization.

Directly across the avenue from Mark Twain's historic boat-shaped house that Twain built and lived in happily with his wife and daughters in his last years, the Hill Center was in an area where notions of transcendentalism, utopian horizons and the arts had thrived. Putting on elaborate plays and pageants with his family for the community, Twain started a Golden age in the arts for Hartford that still underlies its long-term tradition and connection to them. Close friends with Joseph Twitchell, Pastor of the nearby Asylum Hill Congregational Church, legend has it they'd often walk to Boston (now two hours away by car) as they ruminated over the philosophies of the day.

Paving the way for a WPA-like arts renaissance in

Hartford in the 1970's, (The WPA, or Works Progress Administration created in 1935 during the Depression in the Roosevelt Administration, employed millions of job seekers in public works projects including artists who created large murals and other civic arts projects), this time in Hartford was an unusual era when insurance companies, corporations and foundations adopted the philosophy of Corporate Social Responsibility towards the community. Their awareness that they must give something back by funding the arts also helped to create the Cooperative.

With timing in our favor, my last step was to query the community of artists if they would commit to work as a team towards presenting visual arts exhibitions, literary and per-forming arts events. Much to my surprise, after putting an ad in the local newspaper for an evening meeting at the Hill Center, a group of sixty artists arrived, eager to begin. Not a practiced public speaker, I had a moment of "drowning in a sea of faces," and the only thing I could think to do was to announce that we should immediately form committees to start its formation. And then, the Asylum Hill Artists' Cooperative (later named Artworks Gallery) was born!

University professors at nearby universities, working art-ists from the community and arts students formed the core of the organization. Endowed with the "can do" attitude from the sixties, with that generation's conviction that new identi-ties for professional lives could be transformed and created, the Cooperative was part of the nation-wide movement that spawned new visibility for community arts across the US. Spearheaded in New York City especially, where artists had taken the future in their hands by starting their own cooperative galleries rather than relying on gallery owners to display and sell their work, it inspired the members of the Connecticut cooperative to jump in and create "Artworks Gallery" that it became a few years later.

An old upholstery factory of 1600 feet near the downtown Civic Center was the physical manifestation of the gallery, where group effort restored it into a pristine gallery space. Through hours of painstakingly removing old needles lodged between wooden floorboards, sanding the entire floor, painting white walls and installing professional track lighting, a handsome exhibition space was created. With large movable panels that created a new look each time for an unheard of twenty-two exhibitions per year, each individual artist took the main responsibility for their exhibitions. Thematic group shows focusing on artistic and political themes of the day, plays by the repertory theatre, and other literary events were consistently attended by the public, making Artworks a popular venue overnight.

This creation of Artworks goes with a special kudo to photographer Siegfried Halus for his tenacity, excitement and credibility that engaged top drawer artists to its membership and spawned heightened arts dialogues and standards for its exhibitions and growth. An internationally and nationally renowned photographer and artist, he gave unstintingly of his time and energy to also organize several significant art exhibitions throughout the state as well as in the Cooperative. Contributing to the arts on all levels, both as an artist and mentor/professor for university students, and creating a series of widely exhibited groundbreaking photography, he also passed on way too early, leaving a prominent legacy and dynamic presence in his wake.

During the Cooperative's early days at the Hill Center, I finished the Articles of Incorporation and gained its 501©3 status as a non-profit organization while the group of artists sponsored exhibits and arts festivals at venues in the city. The cooperative became an immediate success, and since our efforts to bring art to the public had worked well, one night I had a strange dream that I had to tame and leash a group of unruly dogs. Because the cooperative's vision had taken off so quickly a few the members saw how it could further their own individual arts careers and sought to take over the leadership, emitting an energy like a pack of untamed dogs, especially when they called a meeting of the membership to do the takeover.

Luckily that action was confronted and quelled, and when we moved to our own space, Artworks Gallery out of the Hill Center, I became its Executive Director, soon to acquire a staff of five through an auspicious windfall from the large CETA (Comprehensive Educational Training Act) grant through which an exhibition coordinator, program director, publicist, grants writer, financial officer and receptionist were hired.

To cope with all these changes, in addition to pursuing a writing degree, I had been studying organizational management at the University of Connecticut in Storrs, Connecticut. When I wound up my decade-long stay in the Northeast, my tenure at Artworks lasted until the early 1980's when I re-located from the East back to California. As a last contribution as founder and Executive Director, I wrote a book entitled *Artworks Gallery: Analysis of a Cooperative System* funded by a grant from the Arts Commission that detailed each of the crucial steps and phases of the organization, adding all its minutes. Documenting its evolution from early beginnings through its developmental stages to more finalized organizational structures, I wanted to offer a model for other beginning organizations around the country that were taking off in this era. It wouldn't have been accomplished without the generous advice of Professor William E. Parker, faculty mentor at the University of Connecticut, a nationally renowned Photo and Art historian, author and writer. Distributed by the Greater Hartford and New York Arts Councils to arts councils and organizations around the country, it was a catalyst to stimulate new community arts efforts.

My final inscription in the book underlines the concept I had innately understood about the teamwork and sense of ownership that had to be shared by all involved that would make the organization successful and created its timeless legacy that lasted for over three decades.

"Because the Cooperative's strength has come from its shared ownership and the investment of resources, skills and hearts of many artists, every artist who has been a member of the Cooperative and those who have served on the staff deserve a vote of thanks for their contribution to the Cooperative and its documentation."

Katya Williamson, Founder, Executive Director

--- 9 ---

Shade Grown Tobacco

Shade Grown Tobacco
"I walked on the land, and through one footstep,
I was reminded of all
the people who had worked it.
The presence of many thousands
can be felt in this valley, the history of their
stories interwoven over time
And stored in the earth."
-KW

It was the Full Moon evening of the spring equinox. Light, pure and glistening, circled the fields of the countryside in Connecticut, turning them into sheets of white water. As my photographer friend Anadel and I approached the Nod Road farm in Avon in Northwestern Connecticut in her blue Audi, we watched the moon flood the farmland more and more intensively, and it was then that we came upon the shade netting spanning the fields that would soon cover new tobacco plants.

Here, in the middle of the night, with no one else around, there was an unbelievable amount of activity: the moon showering light on the nets, the nets reflecting it back to the sky, the wind making the nets puff up like voluminous sails. It was a symphony produced by nature between the earth and sky with a great sense of expectancy.

On exploratory rides on winding back roads that were like nowhere else but in New England, I wasn't expecting to have my breath taken away that night. A friend from Hartford's close-knit artist community who was a photographer graduated from the Rochester Institute of Technology, Anadel and I, a writer, who had been itching to do more creative writing while directing a demanding artists' cooperative, had often talked of sharing our mutual skills to bring about a historical documentary project that would feature the state. But we hadn't landed on a subject. Now, were these fields and what they represented through three hundred years of history and folklore staring us in the face?

I'd had an astrological reading a few weeks before from a gifted astrologer who had told me one significant thing: "Whatever you try now, it will succeed." I must have mentioned this to Anadel, and buoyant from that full moon night, we decided the next day we would call three tobacco enterprises. If all three said they weren't interested in a project that recorded for posterity their farms, history, and field workers, we had tried our best, and would eventually find something else to document. After all, what did we have to lose?

When Hartmann Tobacco was reached as the first step, they were supportive of the documentation, but its representative said, "You're already three years too late. That's when we went out of business." It was clear that if we didn't start the documentation then, a great deal of tobacco legends and lore plus the stories of its people would be permanently lost. The next tobacco company representative said the same thing. So maybe this wasn't going to work, but it had been worth a try.

Then we made our third call.

It was to Jan Carville, a descendant of those who came to settle the Connecticut Valley with Thomas Hooker in the 1700's. Coincidentally, she and her husband Don managed the very farm we had been riveted by that full moon evening. "Sure, come on over," she said, "and I'll do what I can to fill you in." We high fived each other and noted that it was a woman, with a pioneering can-do spirit, who had finally opened the possibility of hallmarking this stature of tobacco in their state's history.

So began the first moments of a project lasting two and a half years funded by the grants and support of corporations, museums, tobacco companies, foundations, and farmers. Spearheaded by the Connecticut Humanities Council its climax was an exhibition and published catalog of photographs and writing presented in the center of downtown Hartford. At the historic Old State House, designed by the illustrious architect Bulfinch in the 1700's, the exhibition would also display collections of historic items that farmers donated for the exhibit, and would be highlighted by a massive installation of white netting they installed from one side of the city square to the other, similar to what Christo, the famous installation artist, had brought to international cities around the world.

A few weeks later in those first months when we received our first grant of $100 from a private party we knew we were on the right road with this project, and so thrilled that we threw the hundred dollar bills up in the air and photographed them as they fell. Perhaps the astrologer's prediction that "anything tried right now, would be a success!" had come true, and following signs by having faith in their outcome had brought about unexpectedly lucrative results.

Immediately that spring through summer we became immersed in the growing season of this ancient plant that was first cultivated by the Indians. Our initial stop was early May to Jan Carville's, where she would show us the nursery where seedlings were incubating. Exuding the same fresh exuberance we were to see in those new plants, Jan took us to witness this beginning step of the growing process, and we walked with her into the dome-shaped greenhouse hovering close to the ground where, wrapped in thick sheets of plastic to hold the heat in, the buildings housed hundreds of these infant tobacco plants. As we entered, I was struck with the purity of oxygen of life just being born ready to spring forth into action in this very short growing season.

Not being a native of long winters, I was always surprised how winter held on there, the fields with deep pockets of cold way past spring that in a few days would be thrust out with the quickly arriving heat of summer. It occurred to me that this was similar to the growing process of tobacco we'd be part of, and here we were, in the silence of the soft breath coming from the early plants right before they and their farmer would start headlong on their speedy journey. Jan explained that farmers tried to get their tobacco planted by Memorial Day, and by mid-August, the crop was harvested, the seeds enduring being born in the cold to be harvested at the most humid, wrenchingly hot time of year.

As we followed the process those summer days, an historian, Margaret Buker Jay, who had been hired by the Humanities Council, would insert historical data alongside the photographs and my narration of the process that would appear in the brochure produced by the end of the project as its lasting record. Covering the history of tobacco starting in the 1700's in colonial times to the present through decades of change, she began with the Indians who grew a small, round-leafed tobacco called 'poke' or 'ottomauch' that was then taken over by a West Indian variety brought to Connecticut from Virginia. Many twists and turns of different crops followed to the present. She also included information about the child labor laws that affected the tobacco industry, and the initial recruiting of southern Blacks and Whites to work in the fields. A significant note in this history is that this was Martin Luther King's first job out of the South in the summer while in college.

It was absolute joy to drive with Anadel on those back roads scouting for shots of the field workers, farmers and special netting landscapes that were plentiful and evocative. Recovering my connection to the earth and the people who worked there was a highlight of the project. Other than being the writer for the project, I was the fund raiser/ grants writer sweating through the application to the Connecticut Humanities Council, and the project was also supported by Anadel's many artistic and filial connections in the state coming from growing up in Norwich in a long-standing family from there.

A real dividend of the project was getting to know all the farmers to watch this season's crop grow with them, and especially being invited into their farmhouses for conversation and apple pie. Stanley and Viola Waldron, Emil Mulnite, and the Arnold Brothers were some of our favorites. Viola's pie was the best that we'd eat as we all looked out the window to watch the tobacco plants growing.

Excerpts of my writing for the brochure reflected this:

Plants Growing—June—South Windsor":

"It is an especially brilliant Alpine day, so special in the East in June. Clear and crisp, the sky is full of motion and the earth is full of swimming green. The tobacco plants are standing straight up. It seems a long time since they had been struggling, in sparse rows, to take root in the soil, but it was only a few week's difference. The lady who owned the house near the small acreage confided that she had been watching the plants and that 'Stanley was going to have a good year this year.' She was living with a sense of anticipation . . .waiting to see how the skies had merged with the earth to produce this year's unique crop."

Our first scouting and writing stop had been on Memorial Day weekend:

Southwick and Granby:

"Sunday morning, already burning heat, intense wind. Anadel is on top of her car, setting up her 8 x 10 camera for an overview shot, the tin of her car buckles, the irrigation pipes spurt arches of water like bridges over canals. Pale skinned homesteaders in the house next to the tobacco field are playing baseball, the kids waving to us, sensing they weren't used to people, all living in a time warp with jets overhead." (Anadel took a photograph of them that is in the archives)

Plants Growing:

"The energy of growth limitless and vast, tobacco plants spanning as far as the eye can see. 'No other plant grows better than this on hot, humid nights; you can watch them grow in inches then,' a farmer said. The thunderheads above are thick-chested with heat, and the plants seem to be waiting below for their rain."

Following this process became an increasingly intimate venture, watching this fast moving plant from birth to harvest and sharing it with the farmers and workers as they scrutinized it day by day. The intimacy escalated during this time with the personal interviews I did with seventeen of those participating, whether they were first-timers or had been tobacco buyers or managers who'd given most of their lives to this agriculture. These interviews still can be obtained through the Oral History Department of the University of Connecticut at Storrs, Connecticut.

Because it was people-run and people-driven from the very beginning, we called the project "Changing Landscape Through People (Connecticut Valley Tobacco)." In some cases, three generations of families grew up working in it, and Richard Newfield, co-owner of Hartman Tobacco Company recounted when interviewed about this documentary project in the *Hartford Courant,* "If you find 500 people in this area over 60 years old, 300 of them would say 'I used to work in tobacco.' They may be presidents of corporations now, but they all once worked in tobacco. Representing an ancient connection to the Earth that the Indians cultivated with their unique understanding of its rich soil, the culture of tobacco has continued to be a colorful part of Connecticut's culture to recent times."

Tying The Plants To The Netting—June—Avon

"The clouds rush over Talcott Mountain on that June day like waterfalls dripping into the South China Sea. They push cool white mist through the netting, mimicking the hanging strings waiting to tie the tobacco plants. Sinuous music rises softly through the high plants as groups of Laotians move quietly through the thick rows—weeding and tying—like a herd of humanity roving over the earth, the latest population to come to be part of it here. Their gentle laughter can be heard in the distance, like white waves on rocks, as the women, shy and modest in Chinese and Indian-looking hats, wrap the plants in spiral motion as if it were an ancient, ritualistic dance.

Against this silence of unified motion there is a bright curiosity and pride. One young man shows us the ribbons hanging on his Walkman that his sister won in a broad jump race at Manchester High School, to him an important symbol of belonging. Like their forerunners in the American melting pot, these Boat people who had traveled a long distance to be here need to feel and know they belong.

'First there were six Laotians,' Don Carville said, 'Then they asked me if they could bring more friends to work, and it was twenty-four people. Then thirty-four. And since their hands are faster than our machines, they've turned this field around in record time." (Anadel's photo of their tying the netting is memorialized in the archives)

"And because we had grown so close to the people and the process of the day-to-day progress of the plant that summer, Anadel and I were surprisingly wrenched when the plants' journeys suddenly ended abruptly."

Harvesting The Plant—August—Avon

"A humid and heavy dust already at 10 a.m. There's frenetic activity on the Nod Road Farm as if time is now running out.

Flowers are plunging through the netting that has swarmed to sub-Sumatran temperatures. Some tobacco stalks, too heavy with their weight, have already fallen over, covered with this dust...it's the beginning of Harvest. Wheel marks in the dirt where carts have been dragged. Teenagers rush to pick the right leaves before they wilt and the smell of tobacco is all over the farm coming from the barns, the plants and air. The smell lingers in the humid stillness."

Broad Leaf Harvest—August—South Windsor

"This broad leaf harvest is stark and primitive, and in this last step we see how like the Indian process it is from when it began centuries ago. Teenage boys, like young Indians, raise their hatchets to cut the plant from its stalk in a single gesture. then they spear the leaves onto pointed lathes that look like arrows shooting from a cannon-like machine. Again and again they puncture the leaves to finally drag them in 50-60 pound bundles to the flatbed truck that takes them to the barn where they will smoke upside down."

After the Harvest—August—Avon

"Burners in the sheds: sizzling light through the barns, the hum and heat of the burners at high noon. The dust moves through the barn as the kids wait in the eaves to put up slats and sew others into sticks. Eventually leaves will be hung upside down to be drained of all life. Hot searing air outside the barns. The first picking, once soft and green, has overnight aged into brown flatness, and the smell of age is pungent in the air. It is hard to watch the growing process from beginning to end, a process that starts slowly, builds momentum very quickly and then ends at the plant's prime. It took us awhile to go back to the fields after this."

Plants Maturing—August—Thralls Farm, Windsor

"At Thrall's Farm, the shadows of the plants backlit through the netting look like Islanders carrying fruit on their heads; I can smell the burnt scent of tobacco. The plants are now maturing into billowing bodies with Spanish skirts as the dirt turns to dust in the heat. These are the fields that were the first to greet travelers flying into Bradley International Airport, like I did so many years ago, surprised and uncomprehending how this white sea of netting could be in a valley, white spanning the hills. The ocean in a valley. At first sight so many years before, I had been reassured to see something this limitless similar to the expansive space of the West. How many others have been caught off-guard by this? Shade netting is truly the unusual landmark in Connecticut, not seen in other Northeastern valleys or anywhere else in the United States. This sight of netting over the landscape, an environment that created sub-Sumatran temperatures for growing broad leaf tobacco for cigars, was the identifying characteristic to all living in or passing through the Connecticut Valley unique to this valley."

Two years after this harvest when the writing had been polished and photographs printed and reprinted for exhibition size and then given to the designer to create the lasting design for the brochure, we finally embarked on the last step of the project, its public exhibition. In the halls of the Old State House, farmers began to bring in their objects and tools used in the process, their aged photographs, and other memorabilia. Those items were housed in glass exhibition cases while other farmers helped to drape the white netting over the buildings in this central square in downtown Hartford, creating an aesthetic exhibition of what was such an integral part of the tobacco process.

I was moved that our efforts had been meaningful when the farmers and their families we had both known and not known came to this grand finale with tears in their eyes and said "You've given us back ourselves!"

In Tribute

You could see him get off the tractor so slowly—something was wrong. It wasn't the usual cheerfulness and gentleness. "No one else can plow this field now," Stanley said, "and even though I just broke three ribs, the field has to be plowed. The man who usually does it doesn't have time now."

Ending Dedication

"These were the people who were guardians of that past world of hard work and dedication to the land. They were the gatekeepers of the countless memories of the pilgrims who came with Thomas Hooker to settle the valley, the Black and White Southerners, the Eastern Europeans, the Jamaicans, the Hispanics and now the Laotians who had all sifted into Connecticut's population and flowed onto its history—all those who shared the same experiences of working the earth, and as they worked the earth, shared the special exuberance of its energy, and its cycles of growth and death and growth."

It is to these people that this project is dedicated.

10

Contact With an Ancient Stone

Leap: From Faith to Empowerment would be incomplete without recounting my first visit in 1985 to Avebury, the largest stone circle in England. There I had a milestone experience of a lifetime through contact with an ancient stone. Giving me strength, insight, and a reclaimed reverence for the earth from this sacred site that some call "the most sacred in the world," this extraordinary occurrence expanded my life in multiple ways and has intrigued readers of *Awakening in Avebury: A Woman's Call to Pilgrimage* (published by St. Stephens Press, Wells, UK in September, 2017).

From Chapter One:
Contact With An Ancient Stone, 1985

A gryphon stared down at me in the cloistered entry wall of Westminster Abbey. On the first day of a transcontinental trip after waiting two decades to return, I ignored the sizzle that came from it towards me.

Back to discover my roots in England with grandparents who had relatively recently migrated from Yorkshire, I couldn't imagine something like this would happen so soon.

I was *supposed* to find the links to this matrilineal side of my heritage in what I presumed would still be the ancient forests of England. There, in the midst of giant magnetic trees only found on this island, Richard the Lionheart, (my favorite character in childhood stories and television programs), was *supposed* to appear through fire and brimstone. Too much Disney, I knew, but I still hoped that Robin Hood and his merry men were also somewhere guarding Sherwood Forest in this green land.

But a gryphon? Sending what felt like charged lightning flashes at me across the hall in one of the most famous buildings in London. Was there a message in all this other than too much jet lag?

What was I searching for, really? Why after visiting as a child in a family that had been stationed in Paris, was I determined to return? Something deep, submerged below the earth, where roots and soil entwined with all the stories and legends from childhood was calling me, myths that had a hold on my subconscious.

I wanted to contact the last of aging relatives before other family stories went with them and to see the church, St. Andrew's, in Gargrave with its tower that dated to 1400 A.D. It was the McKell family church they had been attending for centuries. Growing up in a Navy family where our church had been a Quonset hut on an island in Hawaii, I craved this ancient tradition.

But a gryphon, where did it come from, and what, if anything, was it trying to tell me? I wiggled out of the room into the next elaborate installation, and put it out of my mind until much later, even after other mysterious connections had been made with England and the earth...

After exploring Yorkshire in our car, with only a short time left in England before leaving for Florence, Italy we hurried back to London. But then, suddenly, Stonehenge jumped off the map. I hesitated, not wanting to be immersed in huge crowds. But my friend insisted, "When are we going to be here again?" Whatever it was that prodded me on at that moment changed the direction of my life: Stonehenge was the gateway and without it, Avebury, the largest stone circle in England, would not have emerged.

We turned the car around and drove several miles towards the Salisbury Plain, and when this famous circle of stones rose into view over large sloping hills in the distance, I was unprepared for how small and fragile it looked. A surge of protectiveness and familiarity swept through me, a surprising and unexpected reaction.

After pulling into the car park, we entered a long tunnel that led to the standing stones, and as we hurried towards them, the wind started to blow so hard we put ponchos over our heads. They were soon too warm when a bright sun returned as quickly as it had left but this quixotic English weather didn't in any way affect the impact of this mythical circle. I walked around it three times, looking for a certain spot in the stones that would say something to me. Finally, there was a moment where two stones appeared to open and close in rapid succession to my mind's eye, and I knew there was an abiding connection.

As I moved closer to this tiny wizened sculpture of stones high on the bare plain, I began to feel a faint stirring of what might have brought me to England in the first place. "But if you think Stonehenge is special," the young guard in a black raincoat said as he came up to us, "then you must go to its sister circle Avebury. People still live in that tiny village that adjoins the largest stone circle in England. And there are animals there as well."

Salisbury Plain had its own rugged beauty, but what he said was intriguing. A stone circle in the middle of a tiny village, people and animals co-habiting with the stones? And not just any stone circle; this was the largest in England. "Let's head for it!" and we rushed to the car.

Fields of grain multiplied as we drove over an hour through Wiltshire to Avebury. The sky seemed to expand over undulating hills that were reminiscent of an ancient inland sea. A car park to the left announced Avebury's presence and we pulled onto its large gravel surface filled with cars and vans. To reach it, everyone had to walk the narrow path under tall leafy trees, so, whether it was intended or not, visitors had to enter this sanctuary after they had paused and reflected about it, and what inspiring edifices might be awaiting them around the corner.

In a white phone booth a British Heritage representative motioned us over and said, "Avebury is full of long avenues and pathways where ceremonies were held as early as 4000 B.C. There's also Silbury Hill that was the largest Iron Age man-made mound in Europe at that time"...He handed us a brochure, looking amused by how dazed we seemed to be from all this information.

I immediately felt something shift as I walked towards these massive cylindrical beings and placed my hands on them. A feeling of a special presence surrounding us overwhelmed me, while at the same time I became more relaxed. The earthy ambience, with sheep standing or laying in ravines and on tops of green ridges, black and white cows munching on the grass, contrasted with the slight sting of nettles from purple thistles that brushed my ankles, made all my senses more alert.

In the distance I noticed a white pub with an impressive thatched roof. Cottages with roses trailing over their fences, a country church, and a post office were further down the street, but what I then spied beyond the pub was another field of ancient stones. And I knew that's where I had to go.

As I advanced towards them, I picked up more literature that described how the stones once marked the land where harvest celebrations and other monumental events in the then Neolithic agricultural communities occurred. In primordial darkness without electric lighting, when the sun finally turned its face back to the earth after long winters, communities would come alive with ceremonies and processions, the land-scape blazing with giant fires.

I pointed towards the stones in the back field to my friend, and yelled "I need to be quiet with these stones." She nodded and I gravitated slowly towards them, passing by families with school children, couples and individuals who had also made the pilgrimage there. Some sat at the edge of the large man-made moat built centuries ago that surrounded the stones in a massive green arc. Others came close to them and put their hands and faces against them with the most sublime smiles on their faces. As we stood in silence, save the chewing of the sheep and cows on the green grass, I could see they were as moved by these stones as I.

Then, in the distance, across the grass that had a par-ticular green glowing color, stood one leviathan all by itself. Its scale was more than massive due to its elaborate exterior of slopes and ridges that were particularly dramatic, and it drew me across the field. Or at least that's the way I would remember it for years to come.

As I got closer to this vertical monolith, I noticed a place I could sit down on it, a nook just right for the human body to lean into. I looked at it again, now in the soft dusk light, and felt that this was a place I could relax for a moment and gain some strength back. As I put my hands on it, I could feel a coolness emanating from the stone that connected with something inside of me.

A soft wind touched my face as I sat down on the stone

and leaned my back on it, watching the passersby and animals. Even though part of me was curious to see who would come by, I also found myself tuning out the crowds to meditate with this stone and its essence.

Then something that had never happened in my life before that I had never experienced on this earthly plain, occurred. The incomprehensible.

From deep within the stone came an electrifying bolt of energy through my back, a clap that reverberated through my whole being. Dumbfounded, I had never felt anything like this, as if I was struck with a gold laser of lightning emanating from this stone. What could possibly have just happened? Why would a stone, of this stature, in the largest stone circle of England, have given me such a thunderbolt?

Something in the stone had wanted to reach me, but why?

I was stunned, disbelieving. Dazed, I sat for a long time. "What just happened?" the words finally adjusted in my brain while my body couldn't stop shaking. It was as if the stone had wanted to "say," in no uncertain terms, "you *must* remember this so you *will* come back someday." So soon we were leaving England; this signal had appeared in the last minutes of my journey there.

Still in a state of astonishment, I trudged to the rendez-vous point, not even mentioning this momentous occurrence to my friend so that I could return to my "normal" self as quickly as possible.

Throughout the long span of time between the memory

of this unbelievable occurrence and my quest to return to England to find this Stone again, I would alternately believe it happened and then not believe it, that *I had just witnessed the physical manifestation of the metaphysical and invisible.* If it had happened to someone else and not me, I wouldn't have believed it. That's why, I realized it **had** to happen to me.

One day, if nothing else, I knew my curiosity would get the best of me, and bring me back to England.

But in that instant of contact between me and the stone, my talismanic path through Britain had begun. The signification had occurred. Now I just had to return. It would take me twelve years. And the gryphon was waiting.

11

Ariadne's Thread

"The events in our lives happen in a sequence in time.
but in their significance to ourselves they find their own
order... the continuous thread of revelation."
Eudora Welty

Heading toward the center of the New York art world as a publicist in the late 1980's, I was ready to cross teeming Soho Avenue. Suddenly, past masses of crowds and cars, I saw a huge sign written in big bold letters that filled a whole wall on a warehouse. Its single word "Ariadne" stopped me. In this mayhem, what did this word inscribed on a giant wooden surface mean? It would not have stayed with me, except that through years afterward it would reappear at random moments in books, letters, and in conversations, as if I was not to forget it.

As a younger adult, I wasn't aware that life was full of synchronicities that would indeed make significant connections through a 'continuous thread of revelation.' Only years later, after I learned more about the Goddess culture, and that the figure of Ariadne was held in great esteem, did I finally understood its significance.

At that moment on Soho Avenue, I was helping a

prominent 1960's California performance artist, Barbara T. Smith from Venice, California, to locate funds for her next series of Avant Garde work. With her partner, the UCLA Professor and Scientist Roy Walford of the famous "Biosphere 2" experiment that had been built into a dome-shaped environment in Oracle, Arizona from 1991-1993, they would trade traditional feminine and masculine roles in their joint project "The 21st Century Odyssey." He would go underground in the Biosphere and record his Persephone-like experiences for two years while she travelled the world presenting performances that identified her Odysseus.

An early fan of hers in this Performance Art movement was Leo Castelli, owner of the prestigious New York gallery at the time. First on our list to contact that day, when we entered the gallery he greeted us in an immaculate grey suit and ushered us into his pristine office, a single red rose on a black desk. "*What can I do for you, Barbara?*" he queried in a heavy Italian accent as if we were having an audience with the Pope.

I admired Barbara for the pioneering spirit she brought to all of her performances, championing risk-taking experiences like an Odysseus. But she also shared her visions to help others realize their own strengths, like Ariadne did for Theseus.

Known throughout history as the mythical heroine in the Labyrinth and the Minotaur story, Ariadne had the ingenuity to save Theseus' life by giving him a ball of red thread to leave at the entrance of the Labyrinth. Then, when he had slayed the horrific Minotaur he would use the thread to find his way back to safety and leave the labyrinth.

This ball of thread symbol has continued throughout mythology and history in many guises for centuries to the current day. Now part of popular culture, the terminology, "Ariadne's thread" has become an acronym as a problem solver for all kinds of situations including simple logic issues, quizzes and chess games. But the common theme of this story is how women, in this case the Goddess Ariadne, have most often gone unrecognized for their heroism and ability to save others, the glory always going to the hero.

Mythologist Barbara Steiger, a specialist of Greek myths, interprets the Ariadne narrative as: "The true hero of this story is Ariadne, not Theseus, and it is to her we must look for the wisdom in the myth. She is clever enough to come up with a way for Theseus to find his way out of the labyrinth. We see this pattern in other major instances in Greek mythology, where it is only through the assistance of a woman that the hero can win the prize and escape to freedom (Jason and Medea, among others, comes to mind)."

A decade after sighting the Ariadne sign in New York City and a few months after my mother's passing on, sensing some kind of torch had been passed to me, I was aboard a shuttle bus returning from the Ghost Ranch in Abiquiu, New Mexico. I'd attended a "Heroine's Journey" workshop with Maureen Murdock , author of the book of that same title. She had been a colleague of Joseph Campbell's at Pacifica

University in California, and when she asked him about the heroine's journey, and why the heroine didn't also go out to take on her quests, he answered that: "The heroine waits for people to come to her." Maureen was unsatisfied with that answer and thus wrote *The Heroine's Journey*.

When a woman riding in the shuttle began to relay her story about taking her first pilgrimage ever into the unknown in Mexico, my whole body prickled. Somehow I knew unconsciously that this was the beginning of my embarking on a much larger similar journey that could forever change the direction of my life but didn't realize that until years later.

When I departed for Glastonbury, England a few months later, it was my first time ever to travel alone over the ocean and then the immersion into the world of the goddess began. Similar to the passage Jean Shinoda Bolen, a Jungian analyst, and author of the *Goddess in Everywoman*, experienced that she wrote about in *Crossing to Avalon*, she spoke of the 'liminal state' when one stands at the 'threshold' of an entirely new awareness, relaying that "it is a period that gnostically feels like a gateway. Significant mythic journeys begin at a juncture when exceptional circumstances initiate a heroic response, when we are neither who we used to be, and yet who we are becoming."

Now learning about the essence of the goddess by connecting with the sacred earth and huge standing stones in Avebury and Glastonbury, it was thirteen years after that unexpectedly sudden and enlightening moment in 1985 when a huge monolith in Avebury made connection with me.

Now this journey would birth a tremulous new part of myself, the one who had always helped others to become creative (such as members in the artists' cooperative in the 1970's, or independent artists, like Barbara Smith in the 1980's and 1990's and numerous visitors to Yellowstone National Park as its writer-in-residence in the early 1990's.) It was not until this solo pilgrimage in 1998 that I became the self I was meant to be at a time of 'quickening,' as Shinoda Bolen described it, "when new life stirs to quicken the divinity within, to experience a 'spiritual awakening.'"

Now immersed in this radical change into a new life, as I awakened to the essence of the goddess and the female archetype, I would re-birth my own self to become the writer and teacher I was meant to be. If one is lucky enough to chart their own inner being in a similar way, they will discover the immense strength that connecting with goddess energy will give them as they embody the stages of the female archetype during their lifetime: the maiden, mother, woman of craft, and the crone.

If I had been more aware in the late 1980's when I saw that sign in SOHO, I would've understood the urgency for contemporary women to allow their innate skills and creativity to come forward in the same way, realizing it is now time to take up the mantle and activate solutions for global emergencies, like Ariadne did for Theseus out of the labyrinth.

"We Women are Volcanoes,"
Ursula Le Guin, well-known author
of Science Fiction and children's books asserts.
"When we speak our truth, our authentic truth,
All maps change and New Mountains are created."

Le Guin coined the term "Mother Tongue," (that she clarified to a graduating class of Bryn Mawr college in 1986) as contrasting to the "Father Tongue," that she saw as the still prevailing language of our society. She perceived the "Father tongue," aka male language, power words, the norm for public presentations in the United States and Western world as dominating the "long-slighted mother tongue, aka the speech of women, relationship language, and even more importantly, 'the language stories are told in."

In an interview with Roshi Joan Halifax, founder of the Upaya Center in Santa Fe, in my six year book project in mid-1990's ,entitled *The Empowered Woman: Mythmaker for the 21st Century*, that I had envisioned to help emerging women gain power through advice from women leaders in our society, she clearly defined this role of women. She declared that in addition to the three already accepted Archetypes of Women as Maiden, Mother and Crone, there is a fourth female archetype, the "Woman of Craft," a revolutionary concept as follows:

"Traditionally, there were three female archetypes:

The Maiden/Virgin, the Mother and the Crone.

I believe there is also a fourth, and that is

The Woman of Craft.
She is the woman who takes her creativity
And turns it toward the healing of the world,
She can be a weaver of text or a weaver of textile.
I think that's where the women of the twenty-first century
Will find themselves:
They will be virgins, mothers, crones and wise women,
And many of them will be
Woman of Craft."

The giant Ariadne sign on that warehouse wall in SOHO signaled the inevitability of women to act as leaders for the larger human collective with their prowess and ingenuity to heal the current world condition. Living through centuries of the patriarchy that has continued to this day to foment war, separation, and "the other," at the expense of the human population and environment, this ability, like Ariadne's, who was once the Great Goddess in the Minoan civilization, speaks loud and clear for the possibilities of change and solution.

In one of my international writing workshops, I once wrote after a particularly moving session of women's writing: "If ever there were to be an important imprint on the planet, it will be through the voices of women, both contemporary and ancient."

May the women of the world take their creativity and abilities as "Women of Craft" and as contemporary Ariadnes and turn them towards the healing of the world.

Llewellyn Vaughn-Lee, Sufi Master, has written in his

book, *The Call and the Echo*:

> *"Life is standing at the edge of an abyss of forgetfulness*
> *waiting for the light of the world to be born.*
> *This birth needs the wisdom of the feminine and for women*
> *to take their place in this time of great potential."*

12

Lost in the Sierras

Our trek to the campsite at Kings Canyon at 8000 feet above tree line started at Bubbs Creek Meadow. As we stood by the car wrestling with camping gear in the late 1980's, we looked in awe at the towering waterfalls and ascents straight up granite trails from the meadow's wide enclosure in the Sierra Mountains.

"My only reservation," I had told David, my graduate school friend who was eleven years younger, "is meeting a bear. I won't go if that would happen."

"They are mostly in Yosemite, further north. We'll be fine," he persisted and finally I relented, wanting to see another unknown part of California's spectacular mountain ranges. The young woman ranger at the entry kiosk was so laissez-faire about the possibility I relaxed even more. "If you see one," she said, "just knock two pans together and they'll back away. They're not grizzlies, you know."

With backpacks containing tents, a camping stove, tools and kitchen utensils, plus David's favorite expresso coffee machine secure on our backs, we climbed the circuitous path through massive schist and gravel curves to pitch tents at the

South Fork of the Kings Canyon River.

However, when I started to make a fire that night in the camping pit, David rushing out of his tent hissed, "Don't do that! It might bring the bears."

"You told me you weren't afraid of them! That they wouldn't be here that much and that you certainly weren't scared!"

"I know, I know" he nodded sheepishly. Once again, he'd pulled my leg. So much for friends like brothers! But we were here now, had climbed these back-breaking trails to this camp-site, so I wasn't about to leave. I had just handed in another final draft of an Art History thesis to the Chair of the Art Department at USC for review. It felt like I had nothing to lose.

After a blissfully quiet night, we started our ascent the next morning to go another 2500 feet up Sphinx Creek Trail, our final goal the summit of the mountain where we'd hopefully see the elusive Sphinx Rock. After rounding steep curves of granite and slippery schist that repeated again and again with scenery becoming more spectacular below, we collapsed at a picnic site near a small bridge. Remarking all morning how wonderful it was there were no others on the trail because it was mid-week and unpopulated, we often ventured off it to experience more fully the remote beauty all around us.

But now as my stamina flagged after scaling the volu-minous heights and curves, the slim mountain goat David couldn't wait to head towards that furthest peak for its spell-binding view. After lunch, he chaffed at the bit to go, and feeling relatively sure about the terrain we had just crossed, I called:

"You go ahead. I'll meet you back below at the picnic site we passed earlier." We had hiked around endlessly repeating curves between similar walls of boulders all morning. That seemed pretty predictable to me.

I started to climb up behind him as he ran ahead but soon lost sight of him. What should be the next course of action, to turn around to meet at our predetermined site, or continue to the final goal? Fatigue overwhelming me, it now wasn't as important to reach the summit as it had been in the first place, and I retraced my steps downward.

But then something went terribly wrong. An obstacle appeared in my path that seemed distinctly different from what I remembered. "What is this giant slab of rock between me and the trail....a ledge of massively piled horizontal schist...?" Later I would know it was called a "glacial moraine," but now suddenly it was an unforeseen obstruction I didn't remember between me and where I wanted to go.

Disoriented, I yelled, "**David! David!**", but the immensity of space and noise of the wind drowned out my voice. Trying to remember the direction from which we had come to navigate myself to our original trail, I started climbing over masses of stone and rock, thinking this had to be the right way to go.

The giant horizontal rows were full of slippery broken schist and finally I just slid down over them taking at least half an hour to maneuver my way to the ground. I was breathless when I reached the bottom.

"How could this have happened?" I was so sure of our

route and the predictability of the trail, I couldn't believe I was in this dilemma. By the time I reached level ground, trying to think more clearly, I still couldn't figure out where I was. Nothing looked familiar, and to make things more difficult, there was no path. Our ascent had appeared so straightforward with David and I together a short time ago; one minute with him and in synch, now suddenly without him, out of earshot. I tried not to panic.

"**D-a-v-i-d**," I called again. No response. I turned around, trying to re-orient myself once more, but then unexpectedly I arrived at what seemed the entryway to a large forest of trees I also didn't remember. As it appeared to be the only way to go to find the way "out," I walked into it.

Quickly surrounded in dense green, I tried once again to re-orient my steps. But the more I tried to find my way out, the more it seemed I got lost. Eventually I realized I was actually going in circles. *Now I couldn't even find where I had just come from*. Where was the entry way? The path back to it was now also gone. I was even more frantic.

"I am really lost....I mean really!"

What was intolerable was true. Completely still, I stopped, trying to get my bearings once again. Off to my right, all that I could see, was a huge pounding waterfall that went all the way down to what I presumed was Bubbs Creek meadow, thousands of feet down. How many? Possibly 10,000 feet? Trying to right myself, I walked to the mountain's edge, and looked over the deep descent through massive trees, forest and rock. "If I can't figure out what else to do, what if I go down the mountain this way and eventually, perhaps, hopefully, I would make it to Bubbs Meadow and then be able to re-contact David by finding people who could help me?"

This was before cellphones. And that view was way, way down. The survival part of my brain kicked in when I imagined I could start climbing bit by bit down by the side of this waterfall and maybe eventually make it to the ground floor of King's Canyon. But I had no water, and hadn't been carrying anything when we started toward the overlook. David had everything in his backpack.

Then, a deeper survival voice came through, "Wait, it could take a long time to get down to the meadow and the footing looks tricky." It would take so much time that I would more than likely have to sleep alone in the dark that night as I made my way down by the side of the waterfall. And what if I became more lost or even hurt? How would a search crew find me?

Panic started to overwhelm. Which was more precarious? Climbing down the mountain by this huge flowing waterfall or continuing to circle in this forest where there seemed no way out? I had now been in the forest for about forty-five minutes. Circling again in another attempt to get out still no exit appeared I finally came to a certain tree I now recognized since I had passed it so many times. I fell against it. I was done. There was no way out and now I was even beyond panic.

Then, out of the blue I heard a voice say:

"Turn Left Here"

I turned on automatic pilot following this direction, and continued walking. Beyond belief, I actually came outside of the forest!! I walked further, and somehow in front of me was the original path AGAIN! To this day, I know I wouldn't be here writing this if that voice had not interceded! Where did it come from? Who or what had spoken to me to guide me out of this danger? I will never forget it.

Holding my stomach in deep breaths of relief, barely believing my luck and sequence of events, I stood there for a few minutes while my whole body shook, finally stopping. Then, realizing that the time I had been lost in the forest meant that light was starting to fade that day, I knew I needed to move more quickly. It would take at least another hour and half to reach the campsite, and I didn't want to do it in the dark!

Scrambling down onto the path's walkway between the large granite boulders, I flew down the path. As the light began to go even faster, I just wanted to get to the camp-ground before nightfall.

Downward, downward, downward I went through terrain that was not as strenuous as uphill, but seemed more interminable than on our hike in the morning. In a limbo of relief, all I craved was water and by the time I arrived at the campsite, my energy was completely spent.

David was still not in sight when I reached our tents. Getting to the bottles of drinking water as my main aim, I threw everything out, food, pots, pans, any miscellaneous items, and after long slow drinks, I grabbed Dr. Bronner's

Peppermint wash with a towel and headed for the rushing stream at the bottom of the campground. I desperately needed to wash my face in cool water to clear this experience out of my mind.

The large stream was so inviting, pure and silver in the late afternoon light, and felt so clean and pure on my skin I almost cried. I had been saved! By a voice! What an amazing experience!

Then I looked up from the water across the stream, my towel in mid-air, and saw a medium-sized black bear staring straight at me.

"Oh, no! Oh no, oh no!" I grabbed my things and ran up the side of the hill towards the tent as fast as I could, remembering that everything was strewn outside it, great pickings for the bear. Along with possibly me.

Having just thrown all belongings out, none of them were protected. Other campers had told us earlier when we arrived the night before that bears made regular rounds through the campgrounds. So food of any kind had to be tied up high in the trees, or stashed securely in tight lidded containers in tents. We had done this the night before, but now there was a bear I had to outrun at any cost.

A scream came from below at what must have been another campsite and I was filled with an atavistic "Oh good, I guess it went that way." But I kept running, running. When I reached the tent and started pushing inside whatever was possible, I knew that it really didn't matter. If the bear came, it would maul whatever it wanted for food and what else? Once again, adrenalized beyond thought, I turned and couldn't believe that what I suddenly saw in a blur was the same bear? How could it have made it so quickly from below and that other campground across the river to be coming now halfway around the circle? Shuffling directly towards me?

There were no pans in sight to bang together, so I reached over to grab the two largest rocks nearby and struck them together. Instinct took over and I shouted "Bad Bear," "Bad Bear" again and again. Something made me shout "Bad"..."Go Away!!!" yelling as loudly as I could, knowing I had to assume dominance over it. There was nowhere to run. It would be way faster than me, no matter what, if I tried to go up a tree or into my tent. "**Bad** Bear," I shouted again and banged the rocks together.

Then for one very long moment, we looked at each other, and I sensed its primal strength, unaware of its raw unconscious power. It swayed back and forth, and the thought "It could really kill me" coursed through me. I just stood there, oddly now beyond fear.

After the long moment, the bear seeming to have an almost hurt look, like "Why is she so pissed off?" it slowly backed away and started to go around the circle the other way, reaching for and checking trees and parcels that had been stored and hung up with ropes. I bent over, my arms at my waist, and tried to breathe again.

Almost immediately it seemed, David strolled into the

campsite. What timing! I jumped at him. "Where were you?" "Why...." "What???" "The only time I meet a bear, you aren't with me! Thanks a whole lot...." On and on, I sputtered. "I don't know if I'll ever forgive you!!"

"I was tracking you on the trail the whole way down the mountain so I knew where you were. I followed your footsteps and knew you were ok." Too little, too late. For some unknown reason, I had to face the bear by myself and know I could, in this once-in-a lifetime experience.

And being lost in the forest? Images of these experiences have often shot through my brain. How was I saved, not once, but twice, in one day in the steep Sierra Mountains? Where did that voice come from that told me finally to go in the right direction? How had that happened? And why did the bear turn and go the other way? In the end, the giant protector mountains of the Western Divide and the unknown caring sources pulled me through.

---● *13* ●---

Teddy Roosevelt's Cabin

Sitting on an old wooden rocker at Teddy Roosevelt's cabin in July, 1990, I finally relaxed at the end of a huge arts endeavor that had spanned the past two years. Near giant cascading Tower Falls in this area named after Roosevelt, the preserver of Yellowstone's timeless landscape, it was the last stop on a mission to find entry as artists into this oldest national park in the world.

After twenty-four months of knocking on doors and seven trips to Yellowstone from Los Angeles, this was the project's final moment. It began when my art colleague Lucy Blake-Elahi and I searched for an art exhibition venue in the Park to illustrate the regeneration of nature after the giant Yellowstone Fires of 1988. One goal of presenting the landmark exhibit in downtown LA entitled "Of Nature and Nation: Yellowstone, Summer of Fire," had been completed in place of the hoped-for venue in Yellowstone, and now just days after its success, we'd returned to the Park with the last curators' fees to say a final good-bye.

From 1988-1990 we'd connected with heads of public and private foundations, arts councils, families of the two Wyoming

Congressmen, and the daughter of the Governor who gave us their support but still hadn't been able to penetrate the bureaucracy of the ivory tower of Yellowstone.

Witnessing the enormous fires during July, 1988 with her family, Lucy had returned to LA determined to create a community of exhibiting artists from the three states surrounding the Park plus those from LA and New York who would speak of nature's regeneration. At the popular Rose café in Westside Venice, CA, she'd outlined how we could bring attention to the resilience of nature through artists' eyes and soon we were travelling long miles through Idaho, Wyoming and Montana, states surrounding the Park to find artists who lived in proximity to it.

Burning large portions of the Park, the cataclysm turned into seven giant firestorms starting that summer in 1988 to be halted only by the falling snow five months later that October.

Through many adventures we discovered local and well-known talent often changing rapidly from travel clothes to more official ones in the back of Lucy's Astro Van for professional meetings. Now in the final step after mounting the large scale art exhibition in 1990 at Security Pacific Bank in LA, the corporation that underwrote its costs and the handsome catalog featuring twenty-six artists, we'd returned one last time to be with Yellowstone's unfathomable beauty.

"Well, this is it," I sighed, looking out wistfully over the landscape, the creak of the rocker getting louder. "We did try!" I mused about the stunning exhibition, "a real scene it was!" On the same street as the Museum of Contemporary Art (MOCA), and the Stegosaurus sculpture by Alexander Calder directly outside Security Pacific's glass building, night lights flashing on the city plaza outside, the opening crowd was effusive.

"But will I ever be back here again?" I closed my eyes and listened to the silence surrounding the Lodgepole pines.

Suddenly Lucy burst onto the porch: "Put on your other clothes!" waving hastily towards the door. "We have a meeting with the Park Superintendent in twenty minutes."

"What?" Almost knocking the rocker over as I jumped out of it, "What are you talking about?"

"I had the thought to make one last call to the Superintendent's Office, and he's waiting to meet us right away."

Throwing on official clothes with adrenaline pumping, we spun out in the Astro Van from the Teddy Roosevelt encampment and roared down the two lane road towards the administrative center of the Park, Mammoth Hot Springs . Near the Northern entrance, with the famous Teddy Roosevelt arch in the distance, the center still held that official formal resonance of once having been an early military encampment in the Park's first days.

Mounting the stairs of its largest governmental building out of breath to Superintendent Bob Barbee's office, we sat down for a moment in the outer office as the young secretary called in to him saying we'd arrived. When ushered into his large imposing office, Barbee looked pleasantly surprised.

"Oh," he said, "My secretary had told me there were two blue-hairs from Pasadena who wanted to see me." First of all, we weren't from Pasadena, and in our forties and fifties, so we just smiled, and with a flourish, I took out and handed him the impressive color catalog Security Pacific had designed and published for the exhibition. After years of asking so many to give us an opening into the Park, I suddenly felt a kind of bravado, and quietly said:

"Well, we came to present you with this special catalog from our exhibit that features Yellowstone and its regeneration of nature after the fires. We wanted to offer it to you and the Park and hope it can go into your archives."

Now even more surprised, he stared at us and then at the catalog, and started thumbing through it, becoming more impressed as he turned each page with its photos of art, artists' statements and my curator's statement for the exhibition. During the fires, his likeness had been hung in effigy in the nearby town of West Yellowstone where townspeople blamed him for continuing to let the fires burn before they started to burn out of control. He looked up and asked: "Why haven't I heard about this before?"

I paused. "I had spoken with your Public Relations officer about having this exhibit in the Park, and she said that the Park wouldn't be interested."

Huffing, as he finished looking at the catalog, he became thoughtful. "Can the two of you come back tomorrow to meet the larger staff? I'd like others to see this." It was hard to remember what else happened. Nodding of course we'd be glad to, we were beyond excitement as we ran back down the stairs in spasms of laughter, punching each other on the shoulder.

Arriving early the next day and dressed very carefully, I was in my favorite turquoise jacket and Lucy had on a sleeveless fuchsia-flowered dress. We walked into a room full of military regalia with portraits of men on the walls towering above us, past Superintendents of the Park staring down in their olive green uniforms.

"Go sit down at the head of the table," I nudged Lucy, and sat to the side a little further down, enjoying this moment as a military junior of positioning ourselves up front in the room as we watched the Head of the Education Department and other high ranking staff file in one by one in their olive green uniforms. Then Barbee arrived, greeting all of them and introduced us.

One of them smiled broadly. The red-headed Park Ranger David Cowan directed the Arts Programs for the Park and performed around the country as the famous painter Thomas Moran whose paintings were instrumental in convincing Congress in the 1870's to create Yellowstone as the oldest national park in the world. Excited about the possibility of expanding the arts program in the Park, he sensed something brewing.

It was clear that Barbee had an idea about how to include us in Yellowstone's ongoing summer activities and the rest of the staff was eager to comply. "We will back in touch with you soon," Barbee said and we all smiled.

Returning in the middle of winter to Yellowstone for more meetings, we side-stepped large female elks, steam coming from their noses, who now assumed they owned the sidewalks of Mammoth in the frigid cold. We also took a harrowing snowmobile ride under huge snow trees dressed in subterranean winter gear, and I was overcome by their magic as they bent into each other. The massive Tower Falls was extraordinarily impressive with its shooting walls of freezing misty water in winter.

Already planning to go to the National Park Service Office in Washington, D.C. in February to see if the exhibition might be viewed at the Park's national venues, we ran into the Head of Education there that was another fortuitous synchronicity keeping our visibility to the forefront.

Soon after, the mail produced an astounding notification, the real prize! As part of the program of free art activities listed in the weekly visitors' newsletter, we were given our own studios in the museum pivotally located at an intersection near the Firehole Meadows (where three of Yellowstone's rivers meet) for six weeks in July-August for the summer of 1991. We were to work with park visitors to write and make art about their impressions of Yellowstone and how nature had impacted them, especially after its regeneration from the fires. It was one year from our meeting with Barbee, and we'd be invited back for two more summers, helping visitors from twenty-six foreign countries, all states, and all ages, to realize their innate creativity and connection to nature.

From these three years of experience, I assembled an anthology of poems from images absorbed from that time of the landscapes, geysers, animals and other astonishing features of Yellowstone entitled "Shards of Yellowstone," my debut as an adult poet, having written as one years before. It was sold by the Yellowstone Association in all its venues and in bookstores around the Park where I did public readings later. When the Yellowstone Museum was built in nearby Gardiner, Montana years later it was placed there by their archivist for their permanent collection.

During those early challenging times, there was no way we could have imagined this life-fulfilling dream that would allow us more immersion in this exquisite nature and our own writing and art paths. Since we had persevered, I always believed serendipity followed us. One episode stands out in my memory: Knocking on countless doors for any openings in Yellowstone, we arrived at the Yellowstone Association headquarters that overlooked the breathtaking Lamar Valley below where their classes were held.

"No, we don't have any opportunity for you two to teach here," the Director said rather abruptly, seeming to imply there would never be opportunities for us to do. But then, all of a sudden, he looked right at me and said "And what do you really want to do?" Mesmerized by the spaciously beautiful valley, I blurted out, surprising even myself: "I want to write from nature like Ralph Waldo Emerson!"

Well, because of Barbee's vision and other opportunities, I was finally able to do that in a studio that viewed the awe-inspiring meadow by the Firehole River and mountains beyond that visitors often remarked looked like a little Yosemite.

Another time, at sunrise near the same overlook of Lamar Valley when we searched for wolves that were being re-introduced into the Park, we witnessed instead an unforgettable sight of elks dancing at dawn.

Yellowstone, this oldest national park in the world that spawned all the others, always remains as a miracle to its many visitors and certainly is for me. One day I will return to bask again in its rushing rivers, experience its astounding beauty and marvel at the array of animals who call it their home.

14

Curator's Statement

Yellowstone National Park, Curator's Statement

From "Nature and Nation, Yellowstone, Summer of Fire"

"*Of Nature and Nation: Yellowstone, Summer of Fire*" was borne of the 1988 fires of Yellowstone National Park. As co-curators, we gathered a core of socially conscious artists from Los Angeles, New York, Wyoming, Idaho and Montana, many of whom had been leaders and advocates of environmental awareness for years.

For these last twenty-two months, a portion of our lives has been focused on that evanescent place at the Northwestern corner of Wyoming. It has been, and will continue to be, an ongoing pulse in our minds and hearts—a symbol of one of the most vital bodies of nature still thriving in these United States. The first National Park in the world, it is at the vanguard of a national park history that includes over 150 parks throughout the world. It is the wilderness, and one of the last surviving intact wildernesses in a national park, in a world where technological landscapes are becoming more and more prevalent.

Trying to encapsulate the essence of this pivotal historical and natural source through an art exhibition has been a challenge, especially when it is "unquantifiable" and should remain that way. What we do know, unequivocally, is that our growth in relationship to it—artistically, spiritually, and ecologically—has been as immeasurable as its vastness.

All around us, we were witness to the indomitable forces of nature, a churning furnace of activity, re-forming the landscape before our eyes. It became very clear that this activity replenishes all beings on the planet, that it is the core of nourishment for all of us. The spirit which abounds in Yellowstone is the spirit of the Nation in its best sense—still raw, open, curious, young. The complexity of issues facing its survival are as complex as the Nation's. When we realized this, the scope of *Of Nature and Nation* spontaneously expanded, addressing the dignity and eloquence of nature which must be preserved in the same way we would want to preserve our national's survival.

Artists have long been recognized for their significant connection to Yellowstone. Painter Thomas Moran and photographer William Henry Jackson depicted its startling beauty and geologic wonders so well in the 1870's that Congress enacted legislation for it to become the very first national park, even before Wyoming was granted statehood. This exhibition's artists are linked to the same tradition of Moran and Jackson, for they have all gone in "search of the landscape," whether symbolic or literal, and then reflected it through their own special powers of cognition, assimilation and communion. Through the use of contemporary language of their time. They have been more concerned with capturing the spirit of Yellowstone and nature in general, than reflecting its actual physical appearance.

Robert Bly, a leading American poet, has pointed out that our society is lacking in Contemporary Warriors who could lead us into new crusades of meaning with new visions. Because artists are visionaries, they can rekindle the idealism that would make our lives and national life full of quality and valor. Our link with the planet, where we live and breathe, is part of that vision. How we act in regards to preserving it is a new form of patriotism, for by connecting with it we are connecting once again with ourselves and the hope for a better future. It is no mistake that a group of artists has come together to create this exhibition, since it is through community—an early American form of communication—that we rediscover our mutual goals. It is the fire which kindles our new visions.

Yellowstone is a small part of the planet, but it is a breathing metaphor of nature's capacity to regenerate. It needs to be protected before it becomes a state of emergency, like other parts of the globe that are in dire circumstances and fragile disarray." --Katya Williamson, Co-Curator

15

The Praying Mantis

When my father was diagnosed with terminal cancer that would take him in a few short months in August, 1996, we four siblings decided to create my parents' home into a hospice and be in charge of their care. In order to have twenty-four hour watches, we included caretakers from the Philippines, so not only were we dealing with the loss of parents (my mother would pass on in 1998) but incorporating a whole new culture into our lives at that precarious time.

Now the nights were getting longer, and the end was drawing near, and in the midst of everything else, one of the caretakers told us about the belief in the Philippines that when someone is making their transition, there will often appear a totem animal or insect that will help guide them to the other side, marking their transition. This was something I'd never heard of before, but anything was plausible then.

Taking the late night shift to give Dad morphine at required times and to watch the blue midnight light as it shifted into dawn, on the Tuesday before the Saturday when he passed on, a praying mantis sailed through the window. It arrived very near to where he lay on his bed on the top floor of the house in Palos Verdes, and in the twenty-eight years that my parents lived there, none of us had ever seen one.

It had a wonderfully bright green woven quality about it, its lime sheen reminiscent of the colors my Auntie Marvel, my father's only sister, wore and selected for most of her furnishings. Sensitized as we were to the Philippine superstition, we didn't immediately remove it from the room, but observed it carefully, even when it moved closer to him.

This was also the night when Dad was getting up out of bed and reaching towards a place in the right hand corner of the room, calling "Ma," It was a name I never knew he called my Grandmother until some months later when I took a trip to his childhood home in Minnesota. There I met Brickie, a woman who lived with the family as a young person who said that was the name her family called her.

From the book *The Mantis Carol*, Sir Laurens Van der Post wrote: "No matter whether insect, bird, animal or human being in Africa (where the Praying Mantis and the Bushmen who first believed in its power hailed from) when the season of return is upon them and the round of flesh and blood on earth is nearing completion and the circle about to be tightly drawn, all living things long to go back also to the place where they were born...All, they say, as the final hour approaches, long to complete the round by joining their own thread of life to the place from which it first began to circle."

During the whole night and following morning the Praying Mantis remained near my father, and as I went in and out of sleep at my post on the floor, I could hear its feet moving inside the lampshade where it had jumped to, making popping sounds as its little legs went up and down.

At some point the next morning when it was back on the bed by my father, I needed to give him the next dose of morphine. But as it was between us, I took the washcloth under it and gently pulled it over to the windowsill where it jumped up to and remained for an hour or two. My last memory of it out of the corner of my eye was that it had taken the posture of a little soldier standing guard at the window before it disappeared. In the midst of so much else going on, all of us who witnessed it were stunned.

But the story doesn't end there. Once she heard about this visitation, my dear friend and agent at the time, Bronwyn Jones (co-author of the "Book of the Runes" series), whose father had a similar career to mine in the U.S. Navy, told me about the amazing book quoted above called *The Mantis Carol*, by Sir Laurens Van Der Post, the esteemed author of countless books and close environmental consultant to Prince Charles. It's about the disappearing Bushmen of South Africa, where he had also grown up, and singled out a lone Bushman who had made his way to the United States to change forever the lives of those he met with his remarkably compassionate being. It is one of the most poetic books about the power of unconditional love I have ever read.

The day I went to say a final good-bye to my Dad in the mortuary was one of the worst days in my life. I called Bronwyn when I returned home and she was in the midst of preparing for her trip to publishers to New York City where one of the proposals she would present was my book of interviews with leading women pioneers entitled *The Empowered Woman: Mythmakers of the Twenty-First Century.*

"Come right over," she said, since she and the artist were working on the design for its cover. How I shifted gears that day I will never know, but maybe that's what the stuff of life is all about. When I arrived, they'd also been discussing the title for the book and suggested I change it. It was not a major difference, but was another radical shift for me that day and actually turned out for the better.

A few weeks later when Bronwyn returned from New York we were waiting in excited anticipation to hear from the editors who had responded enthusiastically to my proposal and then she said, "Oh, I can't believe I forgot to tell you what happened. About the Mantis!" When she said that everything on her garden balcony seemed to shift around me, as I somehow knew the foretelling of another surreal experience was at hand.

During her presentations in the city, she'd also been given the gift of an intuitive reading and was sitting in a chair on the 42nd floor of a high rise building in mid-town Manhattan. As the intuitive was completing the part in the reading about her connections with her parents, a Praying Mantis suddenly flew through the half-opened window, landing in her hair. The reader gasped, "What's that in your hair?"

Bronwyn reached up, and slowly took out the large insect. On the top floor of a high-rise building in the middle of a bustling city, they stared at it in amazement. When she pulled it out of her hair and started to turn it over in her hands so she could see it more closely, the other woman grabbed it and threw it out the window.

Sensing extraordinary ramifications beyond understanding, we've pondered these visitations of the Praying Mantis to this day. There were other comforting miracles surrounding Dad's departure, views into a world I never knew existed before his passage that demonstrated the realm of our existence isn't as separated from other dimensions as we may think. Even though we may not be able to "see" them, it doesn't mean they don't exist.

Another quote from *The Mantis Carol* captures the significance of the Praying Mantis story that we'd experienced not once but twice:

"...An air of the mysterious must remain because of the inevitable limitation of words in expressing the inexpressible. Awareness and articulation are not synonymous. Each one of us is aware of far more than we can ever express. We all know more than we allow ourselves to know. Yet those who can persuade themselves to be guided in the pursuit of the totality of truth find themselves rewarded not so much by a surrender of any part of the essential mystery, as by its transformation into something accessible as living wonder."

16

Dad's Funeral

Years later, even as I write this, I still can't believe it. We arrived forty-five minutes late for my father's funeral. If someone had told me years before this would happen, it would have been inconceivable.

The day began by picking up flowers at Conroy's flower shop on Venice Boulevard, surreal because it seemed so pedestrian to be buying flowers on a large boulevard in Los Angeles where no one in the shop knew how momentous this day was.

But when I stepped out of the car at my parents' home in Palos Verdes, I was stopped by the sight of a single red rose someone had left on the sidewalk in front of the house. Our family would never know who left it there, or how it came to be placed on just that day. But we learned after his passing that he, always friendly to new people moving in, was well-liked in the neighborhood. This was unusual in a block of Japanese, Iranians, Israelis, Greeks and Americans where most neighbors didn't know each other. It was a single, long-stemmed red rose for my father, a man nicknamed "Red." Whoever put it there couldn't have known this symbolism, but the name followed him from Annapolis through his long Navy career, my mother always calling him that.

The first mistake was to hire a limousine from the Torrance mortuary. Concerned for our mother's fragile health we had decided this was the most comfortable way for her to travel. My sister and I arrived early to help her get ready while a male friend swished my father's military sword in the air, imagining past glories. As I picked out red roses from her garden for the event, it was almost as poignant as when she entered the room to go, dressed in red, white and blue.

Attempting to be in good spirits in the limousine, we reminisced with the driver about the blues in New Orleans, sang and made jokes. What does one do on the way to their only father's funeral? But, then, the impossible happened. Construction was heavy on the freeway, the driver got lost, and the limo went around and around in circles in Riverside.

In the sudden quiet, we realized minutes were ticking away and we were late, and then even more late. After an unfathomable forty-five minutes, we arrived at the cemetery in consuming summer heat to a funeral party waiting in 109 degrees. Near the "Interment Center for Committal A" they had heard taps played over and over again for the four men buried at the same time in military tradition. "If I heard taps once again," my brother said, "I was going to scream."

The octogenarian veterans commissioned to do the taps and 21-gun salute for my father were sweltering also, but they had hung in there, soldiers every one.

Then the Lutheran chaplain (my father's Norwegian

family had founded a Lutheran church in Minnesota, a coincidence that didn't go unnoticed) gave me the ultimatum: "You have fifteen minutes for this funeral." Stunned, after carefully planning the ceremony for days and selecting many poems to be read, I shuffled through them to cut them down to only two. Alluding to the sea where Dad had spent so much time, I chose "When You Go Down to The Sea" by Robert Louis Stevenson and then the most famous war poem of all time from World

War I, "In Flanders Fields," about the red poppies that remained after the battles and carnage ended there. The sea poem, because my father, part of the lineage of sea captains and widows walks with wives waiting for years for them to return, was as emblematic as the other touting the incomprehensibility of war. And now my father would be back with the men again, with whom he had shared, it seemed, the most dramatic life and death moments of his life, even though he never spoke about them.

Following the reading of the poems, the sound of taps pierced the silence with the cacophony of the twenty-gun salute. When my mother quietly accepted the flag that had been ceremoniously wrapped by the veterans with the blank shells inside, the moment stopped. And when one of the elderly soldiers in his veteran's hat with its badges and pointed corners limped over to me after the ceremony and said "Here is one of the poppies for you," handing me an artificial red one, I choked up again.

The crowd then followed the wooden coffin as it was

rolled to the stopping point where they were each given a red rose from the garden to place on it, and it was another coincidence that there were exactly enough roses for the amount of people who had come to the funeral.

Because of military regulations, we couldn't go where the coffin would be buried, another unexpected occurrence as it was eventually to be laid in the ground at a much later date further away. So many veterans wanted to be buried in this last Western cemetery that areas were being rapidly cleared for burial and places for burial could not be prepared quickly enough, so the coffin was placed in the dirt where huge trucks still gouged holes in the earth for them. Because we hadn't been able to go where the coffin would be lowered into the ground, it was a relief when visiting the burial site years later to see that it was surrounded by thick green grass.

Finally, we started to make the journey home as my mother, her caretaker, my sister, companion and I climbed back into the limousine. But, just a few minutes later, the unmentionable happened again! A loud cracking sound came from the rear of the limo that had also happened as we arrived at the funeral. I had thought to mention it then, but it was soon out of mind as we hastened to the waiting people for the ceremony.

Right then and there, the limo broke down on the large eight lane 605 freeway! As the driver inched us across three lanes of speeding traffic to the shoulder, I remembered I'd overheard him mention it to another attendant from the mortuary at the funeral but they hadn't acted on it. Even with this trek across speeding lanes of traffic and waiting in the heat for the next limousine, to her credit my mother maintained her poise. How could this day have turned into such a calamity, especially after their fifty-eight years together?

When I called the mortuary the next day sputtering in no uncertain terms our upset about these huge mishaps, needless to say there was no charge for the limousine! We have often wondered if the driver kept his job.

Days later, on a Santa Monica beach, I couldn't get out of my mind how these many stunning twists of fate had happened. Mulling it over again and again, I asked: *"What did it mean?" "Why us?" "Why my father?"*

Never in my wildest imagination could I have conjured up this permanent memory in the annals of my family.

Feet wet from waves after stepping on small shells half in and out of the sand, I looked down on a nearby sandbar and saw an extremely rare white sand dollar. I had walked this beach for many years and had never seen one so well composed. Known for the "tiny wings" inside formed from little white shell-bones when the shell is cracked open, their legend says they represent the wings of the Divine.

Sunset colors shifted in the sky behind me, and I turned it over to marvel at it, so thrilled how intact it was. A rare treasure! But, then, suddenly it broke into several pieces! I could have sworn it wasn't that fragile when I picked it up, and I just stood there with it in my hands, uncomprehending. Here was yet another unexpected twist of fate that could be added to our family's funeral pyre! But then came, from somewhere as if in my father's words, this message:

"This is the lesson: Remember, Life – it all goes by very quickly. Everything changes instantly, quickly and unexpectedly. Look what happened at the funeral. Life and opportunity are very short, shorter than you can imagine."

Live in this instant. ***Wake Up!***

"Simplicity and impermanence."

Dad, always the teacher, had given us this one last special lesson that had happened in so many ways throughout this memorial experience.

Thank you, Dad.

17

The Norwegian Lutheran Church

On a cold blustery night in late October, I gazed up at a Norwegian Lutheran church and its tall steeple in the backwoods of Minnesota. Was it *the* one my forebears had started in the late 1800's? I'd had to pick a needle out of a haystack to find it in the records at the Blue Earth County Courthouse in Mankato, Minnesota, the focus of the only remaining story about the Norwegian side of my family (my Father's Fathers). It was a great source of pride for they had founded it with others upon arrival to America.

To top it off, the night of this search was coincidentally Halloween, known also as Samhain to the Celts, or "All Soul's Day and Night", including the "Dia de los Muertos," Day of the Dead Mexican tradition. A night shrouded in mystery when supposedly the veil is thinnest between the worlds of those living and departed, it couldn't have been more appropriate.

Picking up the trail of family stories a few months after my father had passed on in 1996 in California, I'd also had other once-in-a-lifetime experiences on this trip when I viewed the great-grandparents' tombstones of both German and Norwegian relatives in two different cemeteries I'd never seen before on the same day.

With my friend Jane, a photographer from Oregon, who was also searching for her family roots in nearby South Dakota, we planned to document our findings in an exhibition honoring these relatives and their history similar to the one I'd completed in the 1980's in Connecticut on the Shade Grown tobacco community. Our plan was to present it at venues in the Midwest and on the West Coast.

When I was younger, my family had driven through Minnesota with a stop at my grandmother's while travelling from one Navy post to another across the country. But this time I was coming for very different reasons, to find my Dad's roots where he'd grown up until he was a young adult.

I had also viewed the little red school house he'd attended that was his most favorite memory with its one classroom for all ages for miles around near the one-stop train station in Pemberton where he was born in 1910. And as the cold wind of early winter swept over me on that vast plain with little in sight for miles except this small town and station, I was struck by the difference of this birthplace to the bulging city and patchwork of freeways of Los Angeles that would become his final home.

The snippet of another story that had always intrigued me was about his father, who, as a grain elevator operator, would assess whether the amount of grain farmers brought in their wagons to the train station was enough, by putting his hand through their barrels. Then it would be stored in the elevators that are still imposing landmarks in the bleakness of the Midwestern plains.

Jane and I also had gone in search of Browns Valley where my father's family finally settled at the border between Minnesota and South Dakota. With its one-horse main street the spitting image of the one in the movie "The Last Picture Show," Browns Valley was a poignant postcard of those small towns with tall tree-lined streets and rapidly vanishing Victorian houses from the last century. And yet, its tight community was one that my father most coveted though he travelled the world in the Navy. When I met a couple there who had been close to the family wearing matching farmer's overalls, the backdrop of the verdant valley behind them out their picture window, I felt like I was in a Norman Rockwell painting.

And then to my surprise, Brickie, the wife, who'd boarded with my Grandmother as a young woman, immediately reached out to hand to me, as if she had been waiting all these years to do so, a relic of my Grandmother's. A white concave dish of china, it was called a "bone dish." And even though it was used as a depository for bones after eating, its greater significance quickly resonated, as the bones of my ancestors reaching across time.

"What if I had never returned to Minnesota to seek out these roots of my father?" but somehow here I was, receiving this unexpected priceless gift! When I told my sister the dish's story back in California as I handed it to her, we couldn't believe it then broke in two. Another gift of mystery from the people of the past?

In Browns Valley, I was also fortunate to meet his math teacher in her nineties who told me about walking to school with him every day, remembering that he had one leg shorter than the other (a sign of family genes, as I also have the same). And in another display of Midwestern hospitality, after showing me my Grandmother's name on the list of those who'd owned the house that was printed on a wooden wall in the garage, the now owner kindly took me to the cemetery to view my grandparents' gravesites. Especially moved because my family hadn't known where they were buried or if they were buried near each other, all I had when I reached into my coat pocket was a eucalyptus button from California and a piece of buffalo hair from Yellowstone that I carefully placed on their tombstones.

After Browns Valley, we'd visited the family farm in Waldorf, MN near the Iowa border. A thriving cattle farm with acreage so large there was a stop sign from one part of it to another, I was awed by what the German/Prussian side of the family had built over the decades. When Cousin Lyle in his eighties, the nephew of my grandmother, was asked if I looked like someone reminiscent in the family, he said, without hesitation, " Oh Yes," and put me up, farm girl style, in a large green combine to harvest corn with his son Guy after directing me to drive the car over the field there.

We'd first experienced droll Minnesota humor when we got lost finding this farm as we walked into a long room of tables in a cafeteria for farm hands to get directions and the group called out as we left: "now don' you come back now, y'hear!" And when Guy said, as I stepped up the huge stairs in the freezing cold into the green machine, "Well you sure know how to come in the right weather," I knew I'd been ribbed once again.

The farm of the Ewalds' (their name meaning "eternal woods" in German) that had been in generations of my father's mother's family was a source of great pride to him. He recounted the story of how my Great grandfather purchased it after moving the family from Berlin in the 1880's. A Civil Engineer who helped design the "Unter den Linden" square in Berlin, when he heard from someone close to Bismarck that he was planning to wage war, he said "I will not have my sons fight in another war" and moved the family to America.

Those laudable sentiments spared the family the Prussian Wars and World War I, while ironically my father went through its vagaries in World War II and the Korean War as executive officer on Navy ships for twelve years. The PTSD he experienced upon return from those times impacted my immediate family for a long time.

The visits to Browns Valley, the farm, cemeteries, the Pemberton one- room schoolhouse and train station all coursed through my mind as we readied ourselves for our last stop, the Norwegian Lutheran Church. Due to our tight schedule, I had had an agonizingly short period of time at the Blue Earth County Courthouse earlier that morning when I choose just one out of literally hundreds of Lutheran churches recorded in the Minnesota countryside.

That night after finding the church (whether it was the right one or not) we were to drive many miles west to Sioux Falls, South Dakota to meet with members of its Arts Council the next morning. The only opportunity to find the church that embraced the history and gravesites of the Norwegian ancestors, to this day I will never know how I managed to select just one. Would it be "the One?" The right one? It seemed almost impossible.

After difficult good-byes to Lyle and his wife Beulah who accompanied us to the German cemetery in Janesville (a name I wouldn't forget since Jane was accompanying me), it didn't take long to become completely lost in the vast array of small roads on the open winter landscape. In a maze of forks and fissures of roads crossing each other and going every which way, we quickly became lost. Finally, we stopped at a small market store in an empty intersection in the vast landscape and there a burly woman driver of school buses dressed in a heavy jacket and scarf directed us: "Go to where the tar meets the dirt!"

"The tar meets the dirt? What?" When we pulled off the tar road onto a dirt road, we found the church a short distance later, and its woman minister came out with just a sweater on to greet while we pulled winter coats more tightly around us. "My husband wondered if this is some kind of Halloween trick?" she laughed. "Two women from out of state looking for the graves of their relatives on just this Halloween night?"

We laughed as we nervously introduced ourselves and then entered the formidable red brick building with its overpowering steeple that seemed out of place isolated on the open flatlands. As I rubbed my hands from the cold, I dared to hope, "can this really be IT?" Starting to walk down its long corridors, I wondered could my ancestors' signatures really be in the church's ledger? Steeled for disappointment, as this could be a wild goose chase, I readied myself to accept whatever happened. "At least we had tried!"

Further and further down the never-ending corridors, occurrences of the past days kept moving through my mind. What had already transpired with loving relatives I'd never met before and experiencing the sights and sounds of my father's childhood across Minnesota was already rare and I knew I'd made the right decision to make this trip from California, whether this was the right church or not. For when would I be here again? Most likely never.

"One takes their chances." I thought as my chest became tighter when we rounded one last corner to the room holding the archives, the minister pulling open a huge heavy door to enter the room.

Walking over to a shelf holding large volumes of elaborate leather bound books of all the records from the church's first days, she slowly lifted one book down from the shelf, and cautiously opened its giant yellowed pages that contained large elaborate scripts of signatures one by one. As we pored through the names, I was impressed with the dignity this script conveyed of the 1800's scrawled in its large ornate letters that reflected the grandeur of Old Europe never to be repeated again. I realized that even if we didn't find the names of the Williamsen family, the trip to this church had been worth it.

Slowly, slowly the minister turned the pages, all of us glued to the signatures of this pointed script on each page. And then, suddenly she let out a whoop of wonder! It was the Impossible, a Miracle! Disbelieving, there were the names of the Williamsens! In large constructed script was the signature of Marcus Williamsen (changed to Williamson sometime later after their arrival to America) followed by all the other names of the family. Right there! In that bold script. Their names were there!!

As overjoyed as we were, she shouted, "They *are* here!" Speechless, we stood in silence. How could this be, the right church had been selected out of literally hundreds of choices in a very short period of time? I was dizzy. How, truly, could this have happened when there were so many to choose from? We continued to stare at each other in this homecoming, knowing that some guidance had certainly intervened to accomplish this goal.

"Well, let's not waste any time, let's find their graves then," the Minister turned and led us out through the doorway to joyfully prowl into the now black graveyard with a light from her flashlight peering into the darkness. Many graves were tilted at various angles with struggling tufts of long grass enshrouding them that continued in row upon row.

And there they were! A large granite tombstone holding many Williamsen names of female and male relatives, one on top of another, on one huge marker of those who had made the voyage across the Atlantic ocean to be in America. Family names, amazingly clear, were also on smaller graves buried nearby from the late 1800's. One that stood out was the grave of a little five year old girl. Since other names were hard to decipher on many of the stones, I wondered, "did she come over on the ship and not make it to the new country like so many others? Or was she taken by an epidemic disease in this country, again like so many others?" Unanswerable questions even though there was an unmistakable presence hovering all around us.

Looking back on this amazing experience, I doubt I could find this church again. But I will always know that a miracle happened to find it in the first place, and that this discovery did indeed happen. One church in the middle of hundreds with no time to choose it as The One. And there the ancestors were, and continue to be, out there somewhere in the vast Minnesota countryside, back in the mists of time.

Saying good-bye was as hard to do as it was with the relatives. Sharing this inexplicable experience, we hugged the Minister with appreciation beyond words, not wanting to part as we headed to the car. And adding to this 'spooky' evening, as if Halloween had to be re-enacted one more time that night, a black cat kept trying and trying to get into our rental car, determined to not be put off. Finally the Minister took it in her arms as we waved good-bye and pulled away from the curb.

As we got to the freeway that would deliver us to Sioux Falls, South Dakota by midnight, all along it were the flashing lights of green combines swathing the entire landscape to help harvest the corn crop through the night. Sensing they were like other beacons of light that had illuminated this trip to guide me to family landmarks, I am still in awe of how I was guided to find this only Norwegian Lutheran Church of my ancestors.

---— 18 ⬤——---

Avebury: The Awakening

Chapter Four
Avebury: The Awakening
From "Awakening in Avebury:
A Woman's Call to Pilgrimage"

From the Red Lion Pub, I had walked into the most prominent area of stones in Avebury towards the two obelisks at its gateway and proceeded towards the field on the right hand side. This was where one could feel how two halves made a greater whole that were also aligned with the broad avenues that had swept up and down the hills beyond for centuries. I had to pass across the road that separated the two halves, and felt as if I was moving through an artery at the heart of Avebury.

When I heard the road had been put through this center of Avebury to possibly weaken its power, I also thought that perhaps it was meant to be there so that those who might never have known of its existence, whizzing by, were still exposed to its amazing presence. Imagining what it must be like, to be driving on the A-4, immersed in the resplendence of its green faraway hills and then to be suddenly confronted by huge monoliths from the ancient past right in front of them as they navigated the sharp curve, what a surprise! What an awakening! I'm sure many drivers had that experience and must have returned to investigate further these rapturous creatures in stone. Not many could stay away once they had witnessed them.

Upon entering this field, I could still hear the sounds of cars roaring past, and also knew that those inside the circle, with their hands or faces resting on the stones, were oblivious. Once inside, one was overtaken by the greater awe and silence of these ancient beings.

The late afternoon light made the green of the grass into an even richer color, and I slowed down to breathe more deeply. Now that I knew the premise of this trip, my search for the ancient stone that had so captivated me in 1985, had come to its conclusion, I felt the earth move even more acutely around me and sensed the stones were in a state of waiting.

I went up to one of the larger ones and rested my check against its wide expanse, feeling a profound sense of peace. To my surprise, a single tear, from my eye to my chin tracked down my face. As I continued to go from one stone to another to say hello, and rest my hands and face on it, each time another tear would come.

"Why am I getting so emotional?"

It was as if each stone emitted such brilliance and strength that I found myself moved beyond words. It was a strength I had never encountered before that felt like the ultimate strength of the universe. Nothing was stronger. I felt it would never go away.

I knew I was coming into contact with something much larger than I had ever previously experienced. "Are these tears over Dad, left from his passing a year ago?" I thought as I reached the next stone and another gentle tear moved slowly down my face. "Or maybe they come from not being able to find *The Stone*?"

As I continued to pass from one stone to another, and the concerns of the outside world began to vanish, it was as if the tears, or rain from my body, took the form of an age-old release that was cleansing. My feet stood in the spiky grass while my hands and body rested on the iron strength I felt would never diminish. With the texture of the stones lightly scratching my cheeks, I began to sense a calm beyond thought and time.

Something began to register: "You are Not Alone. You were never alone."

I walked to another stone. **"We will always be here for you,"** it continued.

I pushed the stones and felt their indomitable strength, and as I wandered to each one in the circle, the voices got louder and then began to sound like a chorus. I had known of the world of the Goddess, but never conceived myself as part of it. I had never encountered Her before, and simply hadn't understood the nature of Her Existence.

As I 'rained' from one stone to another, I slowly began to understand the gift from Avebury in 1985 twelve years before. It had been the reason for my return so I could experience this new awareness and greater meaning.

The intensity I had felt over the passage of my parents in past months, on either side of the horizon line of my life of half a century, was in this moment now transforming into the acute awareness on this field of the earth and the Mother. It would take me a long time to absorb the enormity of this experience:

For the first time in my life, the "Mother,"
All earth, all song, air and life, had appeared to me.

I sat down for a moment and wiped my hands over smooth patches of grass, careful not to touch the thistles and stared at the sheep imperturbable in the ravine. As I tried to ground myself back into "reality," I knew I had always been part of this essence. It existed in my communion with nature as a child, but I had stayed away from the word "Goddess" for perhaps it been too charged, and in retrospect, I didn't have any real basis for understanding what it meant. It was not until I set foot on English soil, where my roots were intertwined with the history of women and the Goddess from ancient times, that I came in contact with what had been buried there for eons.

A part of my subconscious was waking up as I tapped into layers of memories: the Female Holocaust of the Dark Ages, the covering over of the matriarchal agricultural societies by patriarchal organized religions and power in the same way that churches had taken up residence next to Yew trees, or over wells and springs all over the country to both glean their sacred energy and try to smother them at the same time.

But now, here, I was surrounded by this energy coming from the earth and the stones, the clear sound of water from nearby wells, the mourning dove in its call, and an inestimable number of openings of Light in the universe.

Not an overly religious person, when I came face-to-face with what felt like the strongest force in the universe, I was in awe. It was now nearing sunset and I had been here for what seemed like hours. I looked around for Chris, my travelling companion and a photographer, and saw her near the Gateway stones, deep in meditation between stone and camera.

The end of this quite uncommon day was fast approaching. I had a casual thought. "What would it be like if I stood in the middle of this large circle of stones?" In the sunset reddening over the hills, I was pulled by an instinct and knew where I had to go. I crossed to the center of the circle of the enormous stones and placed my feet there.

Looking around me at all the special stones I had visited that day, I was overcome with gratitude and moved by their presence that had withstood so many tests of time to still be there. Mist was now gathering and the sky drew darker, then suddenly long slants of light appeared.

Not knowing why, I lifted my arms, and spun them around me, standing afterwards for a long moment. Involved in their own musings, the others on the field didn't even notice me as the almost full moon started to rise and brought a new brightness to the sky. Then, all of a sudden, I felt the entire circle of stones move like a wheel around me and a loud "hummm" like an "OM" sound came as if the stones had become an orchestra, and I was their tone.

Hearing and re-hearing this sound, I stood for a long moment. It was then that I knew that "the Stone" had been like a *key in the piano* that had led me on to this larger orchestra, and that this wheel had a most alive and electric energy.

And I knew the Mother existed, as She always had, and Always Would Be.

19

The Voice That Led Me On

"The Pilgrimage to Glastonbury, 1998" and "Stranded in Bath: Was the Pilgrimage Already Over?"

When an emphatic voice pronounced soon after my mother's passing in January, 1998: "Go back to Glastonbury *before you do anything else* and work in sound," I was more than startled. Where did it come from? How could it be so loud? What did it mean? The only other time I'd heard one so convincing was when I got lost in the forests of Kings Canyon. Then it said, "Turn left here," and prevented me from certain disaster.

I had been introduced to Glastonbury, a small village town in the Southwest of England for only three days before, slightly aware of this historically prominent site with legends of Jesus and his Uncle Joseph of Arimathea naming it "the holiest erthe of England." Since earliest times, the meeting ground of religious and philosophic groups with pioneering visions, it is now home for new age healers and spiritual residents, the site of the famous music festival, "The Glastonbury Music Festival."

Before embarking on this trip there was still time to

convince others to go with me, but no one was available. I was meant to go alone, more vulnerable than usual with both parents just passed and the recent sale of a twenty-eight year home. But the voice was adamant to go on this path I could have easily not taken into deeper Celtic spiritual realms.

Now decades years later in the wake of publishing *Awakening in Avebury: A Woman's Call to Pilgrimage*, (the following are excerpts from its chapters) I still hear that adamant voice as if it were yesterday. It had been a fifty-fifty proposition whether I'd ever return again, but at its behest, this destiny opened for me.

Chapter Eight
"The Pilgrimage to Glastonbury in 1998"

"Changed Priorities Ahead." When Chris, the photographer friend who had introduced me to Glastonbury and I had walked down Chilkwell Street the year before, we'd laughed at this traffic sign that made no sense to us. It was funny then, but now, as I was on my way to LAX in a taxi to return alone to Glastonbury, it took on a more significant meaning. I was on a journey where new priorities ahead I couldn't have imagined a year ago were taking my life in new directions.

When my mother passed on earlier in the year in January, a voice immediately said: "Before you do anything else, you must go back to Glastonbury and work in sound." I tried to ignore it, but it was insistent. With the deaths of both parents within eighteen months of each other, my life unexpectedly felt like a blank slate again.

In the window seat on the plane, I communed with the water below, the stars above, and the bright half moon. I had flown through the night also on the last trip to England, thinking of my father and his passage less than a year before as I looked at the moon over the water. This time, I was sharing this ritual with my mother and another moon. Dawn was radiant after the dark seas, with Ireland, the first sight of green, becoming brighter in the sun in the morning light.

When I disembarked from the plane, I realized that the jet lag pills that were supposed to help someone *not* have jet lag were making it worse. Feeling pretty woozy, I had been so busy I hadn't decided what to do for the next twelve hours before I took a bus to Glastonbury. Where would I feel most comfortable for that duration? The British Museum had been a haven on the 1985 trip, so I lined up in the queue for a taxi and soon was in a shiny black cab with a round top engulfed in traffic coming at us from what felt like the wrong direction.

Little did I know that when the taxi driver pulled up to the curb across from the museum, the most dangerous moment in my stay in London was about to happen. Getting out of the taxi, I planned to meet the driver at an appointed time, and grabbed my things to cross the street. The light changed and I took my first step across the street. "Get back immediately!" sounded in my head. I jumped back when a car speeding from the direction I hadn't expected lunged right past me in the exact spot where I would have been standing.

"Geez, Louise," I exclaimed and had trouble breathing. I'd just done what scores of other tourists had succumbed to. Jet lagged, getting my bearings, I was among those who the words on the sidewalk in white paint with arrows pointing this way and that had been written for, to warn us that traffic came from a different way we were used to, and be even more alert. Learning later that an American woman tourist had been killed on her first day in London in just that way, this trip had come close to being over right then and there. Something had guided me to safety, and I took note of that in my bewilderment.

Years before in 1985, when my friend Kath and I had stayed in London for the last week of our trip, I'd visited the Egyptian section often. I'd walk by the two sphinxes at the entrance and spent time absorbing them. Now thirteen years later, they were still there! Sculpted from roseate marble, impassive, regal, they reclined with the same ferocious elegance of years before. As I neared them, they seemed to say: "Where have you been? We've been here all along. We remember you." They sat on massive haunches with paws larger than half a human's body looking straight ahead. For all their nobility, there was a diffused softness to their features.

Two prescient beings who were hosts to the treasures of the world that had excited me since childhood, they looked at me with warmth and wisdom, and I felt like curling up on their laps and falling asleep. I finally moved past them to look at the Rosetta stone that was another major museum attraction.

"Imagine that it took only one person to break the code of hieroglyphics," I thought, impressed. "What would have happened if the Frenchman had not been able to do it and we as humanity were never to have access to the Egyptian Book of the Dead?" This was why I had always loved museums; my mind was being stimulated in so many directions that finally the jet lag was wearing off.

Hundreds of different Egyptian dynasties were represented as I walked past mastabas and columns from various kingdoms. Another left turn brought me to the flying bulls that that had been gatekeepers of ancient Sumerian cities, the bull-horses serving as emissaries to other worlds. As they stood at the entry of a long narrow room, a wind seemed to rush through their open wings. Each time I was able to visit these Assyrian, Sumerian, Mesopotamian, Greek and Egyptian exhibits, I felt privileged to be in contact with something from the past that was so unrelated to our contemporary times.

"These are our cultural parents," thinking that without these touchstones, our civilization would not exist in the way it is today.

Back at Heathrow, there were elevators, curving corridors, and moving escalators to take in stride on the way to the bus terminal, and when I climbed aboard the bus for this final part of the now twenty-five hour journey, I was more than relieved. The windshield wiper scraped back and forth, back and forth through the bleakness of the night, the rain for the next three hours making me contemplative.

I remembered the unexpected letter I received from Anthea, the owner of the Heart Centred B & B where I would be staying: "Don't worry about bringing wellies for the mud and rain. I'll have a pair for you so that you can hike above Glastonbury in the early morning, one of the best ways to experience it," she had written, offering to escort me on paths through farmers' fields.

"This was another instance of Glastonbury synchronicity," I reflected. "Here I was coming scared and alone and she had made the effort to write me in advance. Like the White Eagle star that bid me adieu last year, there's been a Glastonbury presence watching over me."

The sky became darker than any I had ever experienced in California, and we seemed to enter into a special night land inhabited with trees of enormous statuesque quality close to the road. I now was in a landscape that couldn't have been more different than the desert and mountains surrounding Los Angeles.

I had arrived!!!

Chapter Nine
Stranded In Bath: Was The Pilgrimage Already Over?

"Bath Spa, leaving in ten minutes;" "London, leaving in fifteen"
The railroad boards over the tracks rapidly clacked out these timetables while I stood in the elaborate Victorian Temple Meads Train Station in Bristol. In a quandary once again after my arrival a week before in Glastonbury, I deliberated: "if I take the train to Bath Spa, it leads to Glastonbury for more investigation, and if I take the train to London, then Heathrow Airport, that leads back to the U.S."

"Why didn't I stay in Glastonbury in the first place?" blazed through my thoughts as I toyed with which way to go. Like most visitors new to Glastonbury, I had mistakenly imagined I could experience what it had to offer in a week pre-arranging a reunion with relatives in the North to scatter some of my mother's ashes in her favorite part of Yorkshire near the Bolton Priory.

I **had** done as the voice directed, "go to Glastonbury and work in sound." But, first my mother. I had wanted to pay her this one last respect and take her ashes to the place of her ancestors. Now I was back in Bristol, feeling lost again. I didn't know anyone in the Southwest of England, and my relatives, with whom I had a heartfelt connection, were now five hundred miles away. The only friend from Los Angeles was at a funeral in nearby Nailsworth. Hardly the time to make a call.

The announcement came again. Which train should I board? Then a small yellow caboose with "Bath Spa" written on its front window, looking like something out of the Yellow Submarine pulled up. Bath had been inviting the year before, both contemporary and historic, so with unfounded optimism, I got on, thinking "I bet I can get to Glastonbury by nightfall."

I was not disappointed as I viewed the seven hills of Bath and Georgian architecture curving over them when our express pulled into the station. "This place has taste," noticing there were no billboards anywhere in sight, just green hills.

Pulling my luggage through iron turnstiles and down dark corridors through the train station, I finally found the tourist bureau, where the official said "You'll have to take two buses to get to Glastonbury, and the first one from here left already."

"Oh no." That meant the night in Bath. The earlier elation moved quickly into exhaustion, but I asked for a list of B & B's and found one still available on the outskirts of the city. I had just enough energy for the taxi ride, checking in, and being ushered to a basement floor with a garden room before the last of my ten day adrenalin high eked out and I crashed.

"What does working in sound really mean?" I woke up with this question permeating my mind the next morning, now more alert. "Why am I still following the instructions of this voice that I don't even understand?" Intrigued, but not sure whether to stay or go back to America, I decided a walk to the center of Bath would help my decision. Lavish red, purple and pink geraniums hung in large planters on every lamppost. Canal boats added to its festive atmosphere with hand-painted vases of colorful swirls and dashes resting on top of the barges.

I walked near the bridge that was the hallmark of the city, and watched as water spilled below in silver whorls in the aqueduct. I looked up at the bridge filled with shops and tea rooms that resembled a miniature Ponte Vecchio in Florence. Somewhere from deep below the sidewalk, I could feel the nascent springs of this spa town.

Still trying to decide, I remembered: "when in doubt, get more information or ask for a sign" so I rang the Glastonbury Tourist bureau.

"Madam," a clipped voice said, "There is only one place in Glastonbury with a room left." When I called the proprietress who told me her name was Isis, and said," Can you hold a minute?" I took a deep breath.

Then she came back on the phone and said, "We have only one room left, and it is the Egyptian Room."

"The Egyptian Room?"

"The Egyptian Room."

I sat down under one of the geranium hanging plants for a moment, holding the phone. *This* was the sign I had been waiting for! The Egyptian wing in the British Museum was a place I had felt drawn to when I arrived in London, the sphinxes were doing their work; I could almost feel the softness of their roseate marble under my hand, their lofty gazes looking at me: "Do it! Do it!" they seemed to say.

"Book me in," I said before I could think again, and realized that I had just signed up for another adventure in Glastonbury.

Another Badgerline bus awaited me at the Bath bus station the next morning and I plunked down near an older woman with short brown hair in a long sleeved blouse and pleated skirt. She moved her bags of groceries and smatterings of other objects out of my way that she had purchased that day. I smiled and she smiled, and asked me in a polite way what I was doing in England. She told me she caught this bus every week from her village between Bath and Wells to do her marketing in Bath, and, as she had asked, I decided to tell her whole story of my journey. Still feeling unused to this new-found path of solo pilgrim, I started to recount my search for ancestral roots that now seemed like so long ago: that in 1985, I had the thunderbolt experience with the Stone, my return to Avebury twelve years later in 1997 in search of this Stone, my awakening then in Avebury to the Goddess and Divine Feminine, and now most recently this return in 1998, with just days ago my visit to Yorkshire up North to distribute my mother's ashes, that I wasn't sure if I should have gone back to the States now, but here I was, on my way to Glastonbury.

When I finished, looking at her to see her reaction, she was quiet for some time, and then as if it took her some effort to say it, she murmured, to my astonishment:

"I admire what you are doing, following this path all alone and in another country. I wish I was doing what you are doing."

I was deeply touched. Here I was, feeling invisible for these last few days, and now a total stranger, a woman from a small country village, had "seen" me and understood the purpose of my journey. If I hadn't traveled solo, I would never have met her or made this connection. "Thank you...." was all I could think to say, and she smiled back at me as she got off at the next stop. I watched her back as she went down a narrow lane bordered by high stonewalls and fields, and then disappeared.

This chance encounter gave me renewed strength, and I couldn't stop thinking about her until we reached the Town Hall of Glastonbury at the bottom of the High Street. Now the last part of this journey would lead to another beginning.

20

Forgiveness is About Letting Go of All Hope for a Better Past
The White Deer

As a leader for ten years in a nationwide women's support group of artists that had taken on the task of learning about sexism, racism and classism while supporting each other to become more visible in the arts, I also led a smaller group that met monthly for their creative empowerment. Those experiences eventually helped me evolve my own style of leadership in a long-term career facilitating retreats, classes and workshops in the US and the UK for the advancement of women's writing.

In the ten years I had not received an invitation to join its select group of women leaders until I returned from Glastonbury in 1998 on my first pilgrimage overseas to England that summer. Excited to spend time with women artists from all around the country who I'd met throughout the years in ancillary workshops in the States, I'd just purchased a shiny white Toyota Corolla that would transport a group from Southern California to Mendocino where the intensive weekend was held. Picking up passengers at the

San Francisco airport after the trip beginning in LA, I drove us on misty roads along the Point Reyes Seashore to finally arrive at a home high above ocean cliffs.

But, when I stepped out of the car after the long day drive to walk towards the house where the weekend would be held, I had no idea this moment would end a major chapter in my life.

Literally taking my first step through the doorway, the founder of the organization greeted me with: "You don't belong here, you should give up your leadership." Shocked and dismayed, I looked over at the colleague who'd invited me and she nodded in agreement. Why then had I been invited in the first place and why were they saying words that made no sense?

I had always been someone who agreed with the Groucho Marx quote "that I didn't want to be a member of any group that would have me as a member." But in this ongoing cadre of peer supporters, we'd spent years rolling up our sleeves together for women's causes and evolution, and so I was even more stunned, especially since none of my smaller group of women artists had been consulted about this decision or asked about my leadership, making me doubly upset and angry.

I lurched out of the house, stumbling onto a path toward a cliff of dark seaweed. Walking into what now looked like a strangulated forest of menacing shaped trees I wondered, "was I once again witnessing the fallacy of peer group movements that made me squeamish in the first place?" Ever since junior high, when cliques formed and students wrote about each other in "slam" books, I hadn't wanted to belong to groups at all.

Even with these rejection buttons pushed, I determined to stay to see others who'd travelled long distances for the next three days. And after the workshop my friend and I had already planned to go to Mt. Shasta and Mt. Lassen before returning to Los Angeles that I didn't want to miss.

From that first appalling moment, my presence in the workshop was met with indifference, the founder falling asleep when I read about my father's passage at an evening reading. Perhaps my way of coping with the grief of my parents' passing for the prior two years had instigated this puzzling confrontation, but I would never know.

Somehow after the workshop, my friend and I made the trip to Mt. Shasta and Mt. Lassen, not speaking about what had happened at the intensive. Mt. Shasta with its glowing white peak of soundless beauty was our first stop where we checked into a rustic motel directly across from the summit.

Wandering through bookstores and shops on small streets reminiscent of those in Glastonbury, I was still downcast when returning that evening to the motel but then I went to the window to look up at the sky. And there, miraculously, was the huge Big Dipper (otherwise known to those in England as Arthur, the Great Bear, reminiscent of King Arthur), that seemed to be right outside the window as it dipped straight down into the cone of Mt. Shasta. An auspicious sign that pointed to a new chapter that started that summer in England, it might mean I was moving on from an older chapter to a new one that this strange experience had foretold.

Mt. Lassen, an austere presence of sweeping volcanic rock and trees, was the next stop, where we hiked with gusto. Then, after a long one over a curving mountain trail, we did a last meditation in the car before heading home. As I woke up slowly from a deep state, I started the engine in the Toyota that was pitched on a steep hill. But when I put it into gear to go down the narrow road, and continued to come out of my blur, I suddenly saw a white deer running down the mountain at unstoppable speed. As the car started to gather momentum and go more quickly, it appeared incredulously that the deer was heading directly to the same spot where we were going. Running diagonally towards us, it was unbelievable that it was in imminent collision with us, and in the brief instant before the crash, I looked numbly into its eyes –it seemed that close—and asked: "Why?"

And she seemed to say: "*Because I had to.*"

I swerved the car to the left, and in the long seconds after my breath had stopped and then started again, the deer miraculously swept beyond the car. Perhaps it had gone instead to the right, but all I could think as this was happening was that this white-as-snow-brand-new-car on its maiden voyage was soon to be demolished!

I have mused many times later: why is this story still coming up from an experience of so many years ago? What was the meaning of the White Deer? Is it continuing to replay a potent message I have yet to understand? And for what reason?"

On a Yogi Tea bag, I had read: "Be kind and compassionate and the whole world will be your friend." In the book *Sacred Contracts* Carolyn Myss speaks about how our lives are influenced by those with whom we've made contracts before we were born; that there have been significant people assigned to help us to grow, as we have also been assigned to others. When these agents are best friends or family members, even though the lessons can bring about transformation, they can also be full of pain and separation. The basic truth of the St. Francis prayer, "better to pardon, than be pardoned" and "better to forgive than be forgiven" has through the years become a credo of compassion for me.

After my friend and I took separate forks in the road, I became more vigilant in assuming leadership and visibility in ways I hadn't attempted before. Now intent on carving my own path of leadership, I took the big step to begin to lead sacred site tours for women writers to the U.S. and U.K. and for decades continued to build my skills in retreats, workshops and classes attended by greater and greater numbers of participants. The new chapter in my life had indeed started that has now lasted for decades.

"Forgiveness is About Giving Up All hope or a Better Past"...
     Years later I came upon these words that were scrawled in bright red lipstick on a bathroom mirror at the dome-shaped Integratron near Joshua Tree, California. Sharing this quote with many since then, I can't think of a better way to

express what we all hope for in our own lives and for others we have impacted along the way, especially when it comes to the difficult and often confusing terrain of forgiving others and ourselves!

**Yes, Forgiveness Is About Giving
Up All Hope for
A Better Past!**

21

Souls Come to Wayfarer's Chapel

On a beach full of driftwood in a half-moon cove, my sister and I commemorated our Dad's birthday two years after his passing. Pulling tawny reeds out of brush to create baskets for him, waves slowly lapping at our feet, we launched them for this Navy captain whose life was so much a part of the sea.

Below Wayfarer's Chapel, an illustrious glass sanctuary on the peninsula designed by the son of Frank Lloyd Wright, my sister fashioned in no time what looked like an ancient Indian basket out of the reeds and as we put it in the water it sailed gloriously out into sparkling surf.

After that, we decided to meet again that night at the unique pointed building to complete our celebration. Sitting way back in the tiny Swedenborgian chapel in silence, I was full of images of the first pilgrimage I'd ever taken alone earlier that summer. There, in Glastonbury, England, I'd encountered a Sound healer who told me to go to Mt. Shasta when I returned to the States to find a shaman teacher. Thinking all shamans were eccentric, when I arrived at that sacred white mountain I chose the card from a bulletin board near the town's holistic bookstore of someone who looked the most like me, contacted her, and we now have had the first of four sessions. Never imagining I could be part of a world that was that unfamiliar to me, I knew I'd made the right decision after the first session.

As the speaker rose to conduct the evening's program at the Chapel, she announced she wanted group participation for her topic on synchronistic experiences. Waving a microphone as she ran up and down the aisle, the energetic blond suddenly lit on me as I squirmed more deeply into the pew. "I can see it in your face," she exclaimed. "You are someone who has had a synchronistic experience."

Frantic, I thought, "OK, I can either pass out now or push this to the edges," and decided *to tell It like it was*. So I blurted out:

"Well, earlier this year my Mother passed on, and when she did, I 'heard' a voice say: '***Before You Do Anything Else***, go back to Glastonbury and work in sound.' I'd never heard a voice that loud or vehement before, or been on a solo pilgrimage, especially overseas, but I forced myself to go there this summer. Anxious and alone, I met a Sound healer who created his own sounds and did hands-on healing with them. There he helped heal my grief with these techniques, and then pointed me in new directions that increased my spiritual awareness.

'Go to Mt. Shasta (that sounded like Manchester in his accent), where those funny looking trees are, and find a shaman to continue your spirit work.' Having no idea what he meant I did see that unusual species of red fir when I arrived in Mt Shasta and drove towards its white cone on top of the mountain. Now I've just returned from starting to work with a shaman, and I am already a completely different person."

Silence followed. The speaker breathed a slow "oh," and quickly turned to someone else. I fell back on the bench, but after the program, three people lined up to say: "We're interested in Shamanism. Can you teach us about it?" Behind them, a Chapel representative approached, "Will you present an evening on this next year?"

Thus, a year later in 1999, on Dad's next birthday anniversary, coincidentally St. Michael's Day in England, September 29th, "Sounds of the Sacred," was birthed when professional artists who were friends-- drummers, actors, singers, musicians and poets—came to perform their interpretations of the sacred. In addition, that same Sound healer arrived all the way from Glastonbury, stunning the audience as he made his healing sounds that resonated throughout the glass chapel.

The group rehearsed through the afternoon for the evening event scheduled on this Tuesday night at 7:00 p.m., but as time got closer, it was clear mid-week traffic on LA freeways had delayed the audience. The longer we waited, the more fidgety I became, and decided to walk down the marble staircase outside the chapel under whispering pines to look at a favorite panoramic view of the Pacific Ocean.

It was then all noise stopped around me and as I looked toward the distant horizon, a sight appeared in the mist that was beyond belief.

For suddenly, in an inexplicable hush in the dark, there was the presence of many souls, mostly American and British, standing as if they had been waiting for this moment to move through this unique glass portal to another dimension. My father was among them in front and as sounds of the sacred had been intoned all afternoon for this climactic performance, they had gathered to make their final passage through this spiritual gateway.

How could this be true? Astonished, I stared at this sight over the ocean and knew that indeed this evening performance would be unlike any other. On that hallowed late September evening, the veils had lifted once again as these souls made their most significant passage.

Coming back into the chapel, I could see there were enough people who'd filled it to start the performances, and as it began, I thought "*I don't think there ever will be another performance quite like 'Sounds of the Sacred' at this chapel above the sea!*"

22

A Call From the Blue Nile

The *Princess of the Nile* circled as the afternoon sun shone down on us on the top deck. It would be a long time before it cleared the locks near Luxor, a number of other cruise liners waiting in tandem in wider arcs to go through them while I was lulled to sleep in a tall straight-back chair.

As I rested, it seemed the mouth of the Nile River expanded behind my right shoulder, moving all the way back to its birthplace on the large African continent. There it was known as the Blue Nile. In my mind's eye, I fleetingly saw a whirling blue color at its starting point. Where was it? Further down in East Africa, maybe Ethiopia? Whatever its mystery, it was a source deeply hidden, crystalline and pure. Called "blue" because it began as a bright blue stream at its nexus, I was struck by it that day.

From its beginnings, it watered the parched continent with its sister, the White Nile, heading from south to north where they joined at Khartoum in the Sudan, then becoming a life-giving river moving up the continent to the Mediterranean Sea. There it formed into a fan-shaped crescent at the mouth of the Mediterranean in ancient Alexandria, becoming a subdued color of green.

The boat moved again in a dramatic turn as I anticipated an intuitive reading by my retreat leader to Egyptian sacred sites on the deck where I was sitting. "She's never wrong," I'd been told, but when the same young woman who'd said that left her crying from a session right before mine, I hesitated: "Do I really want to do this?"

The boat went into another slower circle as I pondered my move into a bungalow in West Los Angeles in the aftermath of both parents' passing, imagining she'd tell me to go "hang some curtains and get back to the mundane details of life," nothing significantly earth shattering.

My reaction to the movement of water behind my shoulder reminded me of times when I'd been in other major life transitions. Throughout adulthood, it most often occurred when I'd arrived at a new spot just travelled to where I'd be overtaken by the sudden impulse to go further, leave my current identity behind and leap into that unknown world just a short distance away. Once was at the tip of Key West looking towards Cuba, another was at the mouth of the Adriatic Sea in Venice, the Doge's Palace behind me, the Byzantine world seductive in front. And years later in the early morning hours at the airport in Nandi on the Fijian islands, I was seized with the longing to follow an entourage of a male dignitary wearing a huge flowing skirt and board a plane with them to unknown Tonga, rather than continue en-route to Australia.

This time, however, the sudden leap came from the words of the reading: "Get ready," the Intuitive said protectively, "Hire a financial consultant and business manager to deal with your investments because your name will be a household word. You are going to write a bestselling book on color and healing."

The winds around us grew stronger, and the blue spark of color re-entered my mind. "What? You must be kidding!" I thought. Then thought again: having been told before that I was a painter in a previous lifetime, maybe that past connection could now be used as an inspiration in my writing, linking one world to another? This was the most unforgettable experience on the tour of Egypt, even though I'd also laid on the floor of the Hathor Temple staring up at stunning images of the Goddess Hathor and chanted in the King's and Queen's Chamber, our group the only ones present after midnight in the Pyramid at Giza.

Even so I put it aside, though I did frequent trips to art stores in LA to glean information about color, and asked artist friends to teach me its nuances. But still the prediction wasn't making any sense.

But shortly after the Nile trip on my return to the U.S. over two bodies of water, the Mediterranean and the Atlantic, two unforgettable dreams about color came to me. One featured the exquisite singing of extraordinary voices as sublime hues of color, not yet revealed or seen on this planet, were unveiled one by one. With peals of laughter also coming from these voices with each new astonishing kaleidoscopic color, it was an incredibly joyful experience, their singing becoming so loud I was afraid my hosts would be awakened. But the lilting sounds stayed in the dream.

Time went by. Years later, I asked this Intuitive again when I returned to England if this vision continued to be true, and she said the potential was still there. Elated on the one hand, I was stumped on the other, fleetingly wishing this could all be over.

A whole decade passed and I was close to giving up hope for any clarification. Then I was finally introduced to an exceptional woman who had had years of exposure to the essence of color as a Color Expert and Creative Consultant for leading corporations. In her role, she had travelled the world to forecast leading fashion trends and returned with insights about color that corporations used for their products and marketing the next year.

But the most amazing coincidence about our meeting was that she had **also** received the same *exact unexpected message at another famous sacred site in the world.* This time it was in Machu Picchu in Peru, and she had the same frisson of excitement and surprise. For years, she had also investigated its possibilities and tried to comprehend how this message should be manifested.

Stunned by this coincidence, we took on the gauntlet to work together researching and investigating numerous sources and contacts as we continued the quest for the meaning of these directions. After focusing on it for a number of years, we've finally concluded that timing is everything, and because now that the awareness of color and its healing potential has currently escalated into greater prominence in contemporary society, it is the right moment for us to create the product we were called upon to do.

Whatever the outcome, I will always remember that the energy coming over my shoulder that day from the Blue Nile at its chrysalis of birth was a revelation, and that combined with the Intuitive's words and the dreams that followed propelled me on this path, now knowing that we can serve as catalysts for the "new healing language of color."

23

Swept Away on a Red Carpet

In a black gown and triangular shaped hat with tassels, I stood in the graduation line for the 2003 MFA Creative Writing degree from Antioch/LA. It was my first since high school at Constitution Hall in Washington, D.C. many years before, and I was thrilled.

I'd missed the BA Ceremony at the University of Connecticut because the professor in the last class of my independent major in Organizational Management and Creative Writing, had given me an assignment I was excited about. I was to write from the perspective of nature in the style of beloved anthropologist Loren Eiseley while crossing the country to move back to California, and thus my summa cum laude degree was in absentia. A first attempt at a Master's degree in California turned out to be in the wrong field, so I was ready to relish this ceremony.

Final confirmation came when the President of Antioch, in long blond tresses, opened her speech by reciting a poem of her favorite poet, e.e.cummings. When I started writing poetry as a teenager he had been my hero, and at this pivotal moment I knew I'd finally selected the right fork in the road with this Master's degree.

In the line of "W's," I stood in front of another student effusive over his just completing "The Pedagogy of Writing" add-on to this degree to learn methods of teaching creative writing. As we moved towards the podium, he spoke so convincingly about its benefits for our careers, that as we got closer to the stage, a light switched on in my head: "I could do this same certificate by teaching in Glastonbury, England!" Since I had already taken women writers on tour there to sacred sites, and had friends now in the U.K., it could be a win-win situation!

To my astonishment, I was seized at this moment by the vision of my beginning the next new chapter in my life! Glastonbury was a mecca for creativity and it was there I could try my teaching wings in another country.

As I walked up the stairs to receive my diploma, this vision literally grew larger and larger in front of my eyes, and as I moved across the stage, I was already unexpectedly in two places at once. Ecstatic at both completing this degree and seeing new possibilities for my teaching writing life, when I moved the tassel from one side of the hat to the other, I was already on my way!

How had this happened so quickly? It was like being swept along on a red carpet, and because I was being swept along in just this way, it felt strangely right.

For weeks prior to getting on the plane, I pondered this sudden course of action. I had taught in different locations in the United States, but across the seas? Even though England had the same language and I had relatives and friends there, I knew it could be quite challenging. But my job at UCLA Extension/Humanities Department was ending simultaneously and my apartment in Los Angeles could be sublet, so it seemed all details were working in favor of this decision.

In only two months' time in March I was on the plane with a place to rent in Glastonbury through June when I'd return to LA to present the outcome of my experience in England at Antioch. I knew that eventually there would be reasons I'd understand why I was to do this that might not be clear now, but I also knew I had to trust.

The friend who had been emphatic that I arrive during the blooming of the daffodils (if only once in my life in the spring ala Wordsworth) picked me up at Heathrow Airport, and as we took off for Glastonbury, we were beyond giddy. I was truly there and had made it across the Atlantic Ocean!

No ushering into a new chapter in one's life, however, is without consequences, as I was to quickly learn. Stopping for our necessary first cup of tea at the concession just out of Heathrow, my friend couldn't hide my luggage in her small car in the only space at the end of the car park. And lo and behold, when we returned, her window had been smashed and my computer had been stolen, a hard knock after such a triumphal arrival.

"It's the work of the men in the white van," the police reported about a group of thugs striking often in parking lots just outside the airport, and after this huge shock and considerable thought later, I came to terms with the fact that the computer had been a repository of my old life in Los Angeles in the aftermath of the deaths of my parents. I was meant to go on into this new life, but I eventually regretted refusing the invitation by a social worker from the police for PTSD counseling to help me get over the experience. Now when I've returned to that area outside Heathrow, I have to admit I always look for the ominous white van to give "the men" a real talking to!

But somehow, even with this huge wrinkle, on that day of arrival we continued to manage taking in the sights and savoring England's illustrious countryside while we couldn't stop laughing since I had truly made this inconceivable leap into a new life.

It also happened to be my birthday, and eventually with a wry sense of humor, I realized it might have not been the best day to arrive. But when we arrived in Glastonbury, our final destination, we joined another friend, also a newcomer in Glastonbury and the UK, to celebrate together at the local favorite restaurant in the village. With pots of daffodils everywhere, we toasted this combined newcomer status as a Londoner who had just decided to move to Glastonbury, and the other Brit arriving permanently after years in the States, and myself. And when the minstrel musicians realized it was my birthday and I had literally just arrived that day, they unpacked their instruments to play "Happy Birthday" and "Yankee Doodle Dandy" over and over again.

The next challenge was to set up the class and begin. After interviews with prospective participants the following week to measure our compatibility, ten women showed up on that first night. In the midst of strangers at the Glastonbury Experience venue, I found myself with the largest set of iron keys I've ever held in my hands on an old wooden staircase that leaned precariously.

With the narrow line behind me, a woman yelled "does anyone have a torch?" down the staircase since there was no way to unlock the door in the darkness. Finally it opened into the Sophia Room, the smell of peat from an old fireplace an ambient welcome. In the centuries' old building with walls the pale blue of peeling paint, the women got out their notebooks and pens, and after introductions, looked at me in anticipation.

Explaining that the process of "writing faster than you can think" I had developed over the years had brought about positive results for many women, I was met with unflinching stares. I knew they had to actually experience this process to understand its benefits, and thankfully at that moment a particularly striking woman with flowing white hair and wide blue eyes clapped her forehead suddenly and said, "I get it! don't think!"

With that, I presented the first exercise: I asked them to pick a spot on the stone wall that ran alongside one length of the room and to write about it without thinking, taking this first inspiration and following its thread for the next ten minutes. Then when they finished this exercise and read it out loud, they were all unilaterally surprised about how good their writing sounded to them and how exhilarating this experience was. Thus began the classes for the next twelve weeks and the sharing of a very special and productive time together. I have to admit, however, that while I sat there watching them work on this first exercise I was contemplating which flight I could take back to the United States the next morning, thinking "how could I have imagined I could do this and actually teach in another country?" First class jitters.

These few months in Glastonbury turned into memorable years of connection with new friends and growth for all of us, with my returning every season for years for our writing together. The pinnacle of this was when my agent in London, who I was put in touch with after going to the London Book Fair on another birthday, convinced the leading Mind, Body and Spirit publisher in England to publish the book called *Bringing the Soul Back Home: Writing in the New Consciousness ("Compass Books," UK)*. A stellar part of that experience for me was including the writing of these Sophia women from exercises we'd done together (most of them previously unpublished writers) while presenting the "writing faster than you can think" process to a larger English-speaking audience worldwide where "Compass Books" distributed the book.

In the following years, many have continued to be lasting friends and writing partners in Glastonbury where eventually a group formed called "The Sophia's," named because of those first classes in the Sophia Room and for Sophia, the Goddess of Wisdom.

And it all began when I walked up those stairs in the graduation line at Antioch and then climbed onto what felt like a red carpet that would bring me to a new world full of the most entrancing possibilities that would shape my teaching for years forward.

—————● *24* ●—————

The St. Francis Dream

April 17, 2013 :The day when I heard from Rachel,
a dear friend and 90 year-old mother figure,
that her writer daughter Joan's last words were:
"Hold On To Your Intentions"

One day, the card "Faith" with the words of Paramahansa Yogananda showed up on my desk. A tattered blue and white square, it had travelled many years with me to distant destinations, and sat on top of a pile of papers upon my return after two weeks. I had forgotten it was there.

"Faith is the intuitive experience of All Truth....(It) is an innate quality of the soul, but in ordinary human beings it is latent. It has to be awakened, nurtured and brought into full manifestation... which brings conscious contact with one's soul, and hence with God...."

After a recent colossal wind storm in Palm Springs that has made the air milder with sunlit Washingtonia fan palms waving softly in the distance, I can ask again: "What Is faith? And why am I spending precious time writing about it?"

Wisdom gained from life experience can't be duplicated, and my wish is to leave a "gift to the future" that will hopefully see others through the darkness when it leans upon them as it has upon me. This is "*The Intention I Want to Hold Onto*."

   One of the best gifts to the future I can offer is this story of once-in-a lifetime dream:

I was in Glastonbury, England, the pillar of philosophic and religious crossroads for centuries, and I call it "The St. Francis Dream:"

   "*It was a dark night, one of first while staying alone at the home of Thelma Moeran, an 85 year-old crystal healer, that overlooked St. John's Church, the largest and most powerful of numerous churches in the village. Thelma's back garden of roses and water features faced its four tall spires that would often turn black and silver in the twilight that I noted once again walking up the stairs to the second level.*

   On that second level was a giant Nicholas Roerch painting of a lean and bedraggled St. Francis twisted in profile with shades of blue.

   A prolific painter and Russian explorer, Roerch was detained from leaving the Himalayas in the 1930's by the Chinese that gave him the opportunity to create several tran-scendent views of those mountains and landscapes. Painting some of the most evocative spiritual images ever witnessed in the history of art, one can only stand in awe of his sublimely mystical work.

   For centuries, St. Francis has been a saintly icon for the world as well as a pervasive presence in religion and folklore of the Southwest. His profound words, simple lifestyle and directions for humanity has always moved me, my twenty-four hours in Assisi profound beyond measure. Thus it was no surprise that after I viewed the painting that night, this dream of transformative challenge would occur.

After a wrenching summer, the offer of Thelma's home for four months where I could write and teach others was a godsend. I stared at the painting one last time as I paused on the stairs to go into the adjoining bedroom, my head facing St. John's Church as I slept.

Then the kind of dream I seldom experience anywhere else but in Glastonbury arrived: "I was on a walkway in a modern sanctuary or monastery whose floors and walls curved in arcs that would eventually meet in a circle. In pairs of two, scholars and philosophers strolled over the immense space speaking quietly. Some wore habits, others didn't. The walls and floors were made of new wood with a blond veneer that lent a peaceful contemporary feel to the rounded dome of the building and its circular walkways.

Then all of a sudden, French doors, made of the same wood, slid open in front of me to the right and the dark outside, where I could see absolutely nothing. Peering out I was terrified because I knew I was supposed to fling myself there into stark blackness. Realizing I also had no shoes on my feet, how could I go into this darkness especially into the black, with no shoes? Panic increasing, I also felt strangely beyond fear.

It seemed I had no choice but to jump and then fall, and in a moment, I plunged into this abyss. But soon after this precarious fall, a pair of brown leather sandals materialized on the ground where I landed. Stunned and surprised, I recognized they were the kind that laced up and around the legs similar to those worn in Biblical times. I slowly wrapped the straps around my legs, put them on and began to walk forward, noting how they looked like the handcrafted sandals many others and I wore in the 1960's counter culture

Then out of this pitch darkness, a faint mid-afternoon sun appeared with a little market town in France or Italy in the distance. I knew to walk towards it, and when I got there, vendors were selling all sorts of wares. I stopped at one where a man offered me a bowl of green noodles.

As he gave it to me, I told him I had $5 back at the sanctuary-monastery from where I had just come from and could pay him if we went back there. He said that was fine because he happened to be driving there anyway in a short time to take a sickly girl to her destination.

When we arrived, we came to the entryway of large sweeping gates that led to the enclosure of the dome structure from which I had originally departed. Composed of the same wood as the arcing walkways I had seen before, it had large gates that swept to the right and the left, and I knew I was supposed to walk through to the right. As I started to enter, I looked over and saw the man from the market take the young blond girl through the gate to the left.

Watching them go, I suddenly understood that by deciding to take the right gateway, instead of the left, signified a milestone marker in my life. I suspected that the young girl had once been me, and now I was moving into another phase of a major spiritual journey that surpassed all expectation."

And so, this journey of terror into pitch darkness and the unknown and then back again into the light had immediately supplied me with the basics, shoes and food. And many years later, when I was in a difficult transition, a friend handed me a bowl of green noodles!

When I returned from England in 2004 a year before this dream to decide whether or not to go back and start a new life there, continuing to teach international women to find their writing voices, I heard: "Get rid of everything." Alarmed by this message, I wondered if it had its source in the resolution I made in 1998 right after my mother passed on, "that soul evolution was now the most important commitment I would make in my life."

Storage full of furniture, art work, books and minutiae was cleared and discarded. China and other treasures from family history, special traditional Japanese Hakata dolls and other precious objects were placed in homes of friends and family. I even sold my car, a contradiction in car-consumed California, but strangely enough, felt immensely "lighter." With the U.K.'s mass transportation, I wouldn't need it anyway.

Being without shoes, facing the unknown through loss, devastation or deprivation, faith invariably comes into play. In the haunting aftermath of awakening from this dream, its essence has echoed through my being since then.

"Who cares if the world is strewn with thorns?
Simply put on the sandals and walk over them.
The sandals are the knowledge that God alone exists."
Ramakrishna

25

White Pods and the Battleship Arizona

*"Life is not measured by the breaths we take,
but by the moments that take our breath away."*

A profusion of colorful flowers swept by lush sweet air always greeted us at sunrise every week day when my brother, sister and I walked barefoot to the ferry that took us to Honolulu.

In pink-stained dawns, we'd ride the half hour boat from a Navy launch pad to another dock, and be met by a bus that drove us to Punahou, one of the earliest missionary schools on O'ahu. It was the 1950's, and the Hawaiian custom of the day was for all to go barefoot in schools and everywhere else, so there we were joined by students who also weren't wearing shoes!

The granddaughter of the famous Hawaiian author Horace Bushnell who wrote about the history and traditions of the islands told me once he confirmed that going barefoot at an early age established a long-lasting connection to Hawaii's red earth, explaining why I've always felt a deep affinity to this land in the Pacific Ocean since I was eight years old.

Our home was Ford Island in the middle of Pearl Harbor where my father was Chief of Staff and as the sun accompanied us on our round trip ferry ride back to the island during those days, we'd pass by the infamous Arizona that went down in World War II only fourteen years before, now moored by the side of the island. Enthralled by the extraordinary nature surrounding us, it would take me years later to remember a sacred event that occurred with me and my siblings, twins five and a half years older, about this ship and the sailors who sank in it in the muddy silt of the harbor.

Each day on our way to and from the ferry we'd also pass a large Banyan tree. With thick branches that reached in every direction, and close to the Arizona, it became a second home for me where I'd spend hours playing on it and climbing its huge trunks. Its lower base was a living room in my imagination and the branches above were places to perch and endlessly look out at the view.

Resting often on these huge wooden perches, I'd play house for hours to my heart's content. Even when called back for dinner to Quarters "L," I never went far from it as I walked home barefoot in the dark past large centipedes but somehow was never stung by them.

When the Arizona was struck down on that tumultuous day, December 7, 1941, the tree wasn't far from it. As children we knew something tragic had happened to the ship that permeated the atmosphere around us, but as life, unheeded, goes on, it wasn't at the forefront of our minds even though it had occurred such a relatively short time before.

Then a black hulk with a whale-like prow sticking out of the water, there was only a simple red boulder in memoriam to it that was placed on a bluff nearby for which my mother and other Navy wives had raised funds. We were told many stories about the searches for the lost men on the ship who could still be in those waters, and because to this day oil slicks and deep underwater quicksand permeate Pearl Harbor, that there were numerous ill-fated attempts to remove remaining bodies on the ship. Hearsay on the island was that at least one diver had been sacrificed into the slick mud and oil in attempts to remove them.

Now a white concave memorial has been built over it, and a large memorial museum commemorating it and the events of World War II has been installed on the water on the Honolulu side facing it. Tourist boats leave from this visitors' center on an hourly basis to go onboard that has become Honolulu's second biggest tourist attraction. Loud speakers on those launches blare out the circumstances of the events and the men's heroism on that fateful day, and when one steps onboard, if they go back to the furthest platform after passing under golden arches with memorial plaques displaying the names of those who perished, one can still see oil seeping unchecked below its hulk in the water.

Attending a particularly poignant December 7th anniversary sixty-six years later at the visitors' center after the band played and taps sounded, I watched the survivors of the Arizona get up to speak and break down in tears as they recounted this most traumatic day in their lives.

Because of a quick change in Navy orders, my family left unexpectedly for Paris, France in the middle of the school year after only a year and a half in paradise. Of all the Navy families who departed the island, my sister and I were told we were one of the few to return years later and I was thrilled to see the special Mother banyan once again. I returned to Hawaii often as an adult, and it was forty-five years later that I came to grips with an astonishing event that could have occurred on the island with my siblings.

In a healing treatment for overall well-being and rejuvenation I'd reserved upon return to O'ahu, one healer at my head and the other at my feet doing Reiki and massage with mystical music playing, I suddenly felt myself go out of body. Very startled to see myself flying high above the blue earth, with it seeming to get further and further away, I couldn't believe this was happening!

"What am I doing here? I'm not ready to leave the Earth yet," was an emphatic reaction throughout my body, especially since I'd never had this kind of an "out of body" experience before. Luckily my instinctive reaction was so strong that I swooshed back to earth right away, and then, where did I return to once I got closer to O'ahu? There I was above Ford Island where the most surprising sight awaited me.

With my sister and brother I was at a favorite intersection that had been a frequent gathering place for neighborhood kids. At a corner area in a red patch of earth near rows of quarters across from another memorable banyan tree, it led down a path to the pool and Officers' Club, and was a most happy place in childhood. Jubilation coursed through me to be back at this special place, where we had played endlessly, even pulling Halloween tricks on passengers passing by on buses that circumambulated the island. It was also where we stood one night together after hearing of the polio epidemic coming to the islands and wondering when it could strike us, seeming to come out of a darkened Hawaiian sky.

Now in this moment, I look incredulously down at the three of us, my brother, sister and I as we seem to be, in extraordinary gestures, carefully carrying, one by one, what looked like large viscous plastic pods from the Arizona. Appearing to be tenderly moving the white containers to place them safely elsewhere off to the left out of sight, we were on a sacred mission.

How could this be? "What were we doing with these 'pods' and where were we placing them? Could those **really** be the 'souls' of the sailors who had long been trapped in the Arizona that we were transporting to a final resting place?"

Who would ever think a 'white pod' would hold a soul, particularly the ones of those who had been so dramatically exited from life years before? And more quixotically, why were we chosen to do this? When I came out of the treatment, I tried to recount these images to the healers, and have never forgotten how touched I was to be so gently moving these very fragile enclosures somewhere, it seemed, out of harm's way.

Perhaps as children and teenagers living close to the Arizona a short time after the dramatic events of 1941, I wondered if this sacred mission of bringing these men's spirits from the sea was coming from a subconscious desire to help years later, or was it partially a reason why my family had been stationed on the Island in the first place? In childhood, travelling from post to post by plane, ship, train, and car, we each had our own St. Christopher medallions for protection, and an early childhood memory was looking at them and noticing how each was a different color: mine was blood red; my brother's was gold yellow; and my sister's turquoise, all talismanic to my eyes.

One watches out for everyone else, families and others in the military, a known but unstated fact that this protection and help is *what one does*, especially for newcomers. That sense of collective community and duty was even stronger on the island, especially with the Arizona the key monument there.

As adults, the three of us have all worked in healing fields in our careers, my sister living again in Hawaii and an expert in the Hawaiian Lomi Lomi healing massage technique, my brother a personal injury lawyer who studied medicine and was thus acquainted with all parts of the body. I learned Reiki, Jin Shin Do, and Sacral Cranial technique while using my healing ability to help numerous writers feel safe as they worked to discover their unique creativity with the model of "writing faster than you can think" technique I developed as a writer-in-residence at Yellowstone National Park.

It was clear that with great care these cherished white pods were being tenderly moved to somewhere sacred and safe. Perhaps the historically close connection of the Arizona and Pearl Harbor and our living in an atmosphere rife with the loss of these men created wishful thinking to help them.

But as this vision has remained clear to me to today,
there is the hope that whatever we were transporting
found its way to a brighter world outside the ship that
still lies heavily buried in Hawaiian waters, with the oil
seeping out of it.
"There are more things in heaven and earth, Horatio,
Than are dreamt of in your philosophy."
Hamlet 1.5.167-8 Hamlet to Horatio

26

The Colors of India

In an inestimable feast of color, I look out the window of my retreat room as the purple of a woman's sari and lemon of another goes by. Orange calla lilies grace the garden in Meherabad while roseate flowers mesh with fuchsia, peeking through white bougainvillea on a tree of orange bark. This overwhelming parade of color fills my eyes at my writing desk from dawn to dusk east of Mumbai at the Meher Retreat Center near Ahmednagar, India.

How did I get here? Especially after only a few short years when introduced to this new spiritual world of Meher Baba ?

"Here are your sandals for when you go to India," Buffy, a devotee I hardly knew thrust a pair of shoes at me at "Baba's home in the West," the Meher Retreat Center in Myrtle Beach, South Carolina. Two years after my introduction to Baba in Glastonbury, I stood with my mouth open in a kitchen area there, feeling like a newbie among all the followers. This trip to my first retreat center in Myrtle Beach, South Carolina from California had been enough of a challenge. But going to India, half-way around the world, what would that mean?

"I'm never going to India," I said flatly, "It's too far away. Its population is huge, I don't know how I could handle the poverty and every friend who has ever been there speaks of its chaos." Already sensing I was as close to heaven on earth as I could be in Myrtle Beach by the ocean near a large glowing lake and miles of pristine white dunes, I had no need to go further. I thanked Buffy, and shoved the thick white sandals in the suitcase, never thinking of them again.

A few days later, in another kitchen where people gathered, a blond woman came over to me and whispered: "There's a scholarship for people to go to India. Given by a woman in honor of her husband who died a few years ago; not many know about it as she doesn't want it to be too public. But here's her name and address."

On a whim, I spontaneously sent the potential donor some of my poetry. She replied that my name could be put on the list for going to India, but there were many before me. That was fine as it mirrored my own ambivalence.

But then, three years later, Patricia, my Meher Baba mentor from Glastonbury, announced she was returning to India, and who would like to go with her? Another carrot. If I were to ever go, I thought, it would be holding onto the coat tails of one who knew India and was well-travelled there. And she wanted to go for three weeks at a time in November when the weather was best and fewer people would be there. Those were my preferences as well.

My life had already opened up to other unforeseen rich journeys. Among them, going to England, teaching and having a book published there were special cornerstones. Did I need more growth in consciousness? The scholarship covered air fare only, so travelling anyway to India continued to be a remote possibility anyway, and I sighed a breath of relief.

But just then another windfall occurred. Only a month before the trip, a staff person from UCLA told me there was a small amount of funds owed to me retroactively that would soon be made available. I called the donor.

"This is surprising, you're at the top of the list!" she exclaimed. Checking again that it was definite since others before me had dropped out unexpectedly, she said, "Yes, for sure you are at the top." Nervous and excited, I heard her say "but if you go, there is one condition."

"Finally, the catch!" I knew it!!!

"To maximize your experience, you can only go there, and must return home right away. No other travel in India." Not believing this was even possibly happening, I didn't have a desire to explore anywhere elsewhere in India anyway. There would be so much to process upon return from an amazing three weeks there, why would I want to go elsewhere?

Imagining the quiet retreat atmosphere retreat would take me deeper into the spiritual realm I was already comfortable with since I'd practiced meditation for years, being there would be a deeply healing three weeks. I was also drawn to experience Meher Baba's final home and resting place, the Samadhi, a tall white marble monument similar to others found in India with a blue cupola that overpowered the landscape. Inside were also memorable paintings of Meher Baba's journey from the 1920's to the 1960's that he'd commissioned by a special artist on all the walls above the tomb that were worth seeing.

So on October 29, 2010 I bit the bullet, and boarded a plane from LAX to Heathrow, where I met Patricia, and we flew onto Mumbai. One last story I pondered on the flight was about a Western woman who'd arrived there, got off the plane, took one look around, and climbed back on it, never to return. I was hoping I wouldn't have the same reaction. But so enthralled crossing the Black Sea and Turkey and other countries I'd never seen before, including the shape of Afghanistan far away out the plane window, I lost all trepidation.

Instead of the poverty and chaos I'd heard about, now every day I was regaled with this "inestimable feast of color" and dignity of the Guajarati and Marathi women in their ongoing parade of aqua, orange and white flowered saris. As they carried blue buckets and bamboo stalks in their hands and reverently swept the arches in the ceilings, they seemed in a rhythmic dance of beauty. As entranced as I was with this feast of color surrounding me, in contrast I wore mostly white, akin to many spiritual followers, both Indians and non-Indians throughout India, not a conscious decision but just because I was drawn to it.

On this large area of the Retreat's land, there were also crafts cooperatives opened by women who spoke with purpose about their helping to change India's economy bolstering other women's' efforts in similar ventures around the country.

In the long meadows leading to the other side of the retreat and the Samadhi, every day a soporific silver mist hung in yellow range grass. Going to the top of the stairs on the upper level of my building in the early mornings, I heard a woman's voice, clear and distinct, singing a Hindi bhajan from the nearby ancient village of Aragaon. Those earliest hours of the morning also brought a man's voice after hers who called devotees to prayer in the Muslim tradition; both religious practices side-by-side.

I witnessed this same side-by-side interaction between women and men wherever I went, whether standing together waiting at bus or train stations, in tandem on motor bikes, or working together in offices and hotels. Women managers at the Meher Center also held leadership positions in financial, spiritual and culinary arenas.

Once, when a younger woman with dark braids in a pink sari momentarily filled the window as she pushed the soft broom into crevices in the ceiling above, I remembered the bright flashes of color of saris in the huge crowds of Mumbai's worst traffic while our driver navigated through tumultuous intersections. All around us, the saris on the women somehow always looked surprisingly clean and artfully wrapped, even if one was sitting on the ground cooking in a pot, the cloth fitted expertly around her body.

Little girls with big dark glasses and fitted caps often sat next to the handle bars in front of their parents on zooming motorcycles, and I watched how a two year-old girl in purple velvet at Meher Baba's Samadhi Tomb put a flower on each of the female devotees' tombs and bowed as if she knew, her black eyes brilliant in her purple shift, exactly what to do.

Watching them and the baby girl in white chenille in the Diwali festivities honoring Krishna (India's Christmas) crawl amongst Sunday celebrators towards the musicians at the retreat center, I felt once again the strength and future presence of women in India. Symbolically fueled by this strong vibration of color everywhere that reflected this inner resolve, one sensed that women wearing these colors could indeed bring about desperately needed change in the economic and social growth of their country.

The booming industries of cooperatives directed by women, the influence of popular female gurus Amma, Mother Meera and the Mother of Oroville, joined with a powerful women president and two women prime ministers throughout the years in government have made significant inroads that are tipping the scale. Governmental officials have declared that Indian woman are playing a pioneering role in establishing new milestones for India's economy, and that if India is to progress and reach new heights it can only be possible when women walk shoulder-to-shoulder politically with men, and social stigmas and restrictions must be lifted.

"India's women are leading a new era of entrepreneurship, innovation and social impact" stated an insight report from Impact Alpha, an investment and financial news bureau providing daily news and "actionable intelligence" for the future. In an article from the news bureau, it asserted that it is accepted truth that the rising social and economic power of women in India is a *global megatrend bigger* than the rise of China and India in the last two decades.

Travelling through miles and miles of slums in Mumbai on the way back to the airport, I suddenly saw one brave flag of bright red faraway on a balcony in one of many beige high rises stacked together. It changed the entire energy of its surrounding environment, and in a heartbeat I understood a major reason why I'd had to make the journey. Like color, the great equalizer that adorns this country in such richness even in pandemonium, I believe the strength and ingenuity of Indian women in their leadership will change conditions critical in the world along with all the others in distant countries. As I had witnessed this first-hand, I know it to be true.

27

The Man with the String

Staying with me all these years is the memory of what happened the next to last day I was in India.

A friend offered to escort me on a special journey outside the retreat center at Meherabad where I'd sequestered myself for my three weeks there, rarely venturing into the mayhem of Ahmednagar, the nearby town with its markets, traffic, cows and chaos. I'd preferred the lush quiet, its environment full of flowers and birdsong in retreat and writing.

But the idea for this day came about when she'd showed me the exquisite wooden carving she owned of a miniature hand that held, when opened, two smaller carvings of a Deva Goddess on the left side, and Ganesh on the right. Both were surrounded in a filigreed Indian ornamentation of flutes and flowers with cobra-like images wrapped around them slithering up their sides in knotted cords of wood. They sat in small window frames held by this prayerful hand one had to open from the outside to discover them. Five fingers were carved on both sides of the hand, all the nails delicately etched at their tops. The middle finger was the tallest, forefinger and ring finger beside it, and little finger and thumb below, all giving it a deeply prayerful presence.

Even though I'd known the minute I'd seen it I had to have one just like it as my final prized possession from India, our journey to acquire it was tumultuous along the way. Rain buffeted our open rickshaw through the ancient village of Aragaon below the retreat center to a meeting point with a fellow Westerner living there who'd take us to one of the few restaurants on a side street in Ahmednagar where the food was safe to eat. When we three blond Western women arrived, all conversation stopped. But the noise resumed when we got to our table to a very tasty meal of Chicken Tikka, a reprieve from the vegetarian food served at the retreat. Chicken and coffee became highly desirable after three weeks!

However, when we returned from the meal on a bus through the bustling center of Ahmednagar, it stopped at what looked like the wrong side of the road from where we'd get another rickshaw for our next destination where we'd buy the precious object. We'd have to cross an immensely crowded busy street to pick it up, and I immediately froze. Acclimated to India, my friends were seemingly unphased by the teeming ox-carts, cows, motorcycles, small cars, and people every-where, and they started to hurtle themselves across it. Numb beyond fear at this spectacle, I screamed above the noise, "Whoa!" tugging on my friend's sleeve. "Wait just a minute." I yelled. "You can't expect me to walk across that....." They halted, huddled around me, gently prodding: "You will be ok," they said, "Just have Faith. It is a test of faith....if you just follow us and our footsteps, if we walk slowly and follow the rhythm of the traffic, we'll be fine."

Not believing they were actually saying this, I yelled as I scanned another way to get safely across the street, "Are you kidding?" I knew if I had to, I'd find a longer way around all this somehow even if it boycotted the trip. My friend looked piercingly into my eyes, and once again repeated, "If you have faith, you will not be hurt. You just follow the rhythm of the traffic."

"Excuse me?" Irritated now with my heart throbbing, "I don't need to prove my faith in this way. It's one thing to believe, but not when it defies all rationality." For some time, we stared at each other and the traffic. What then pushed me ahead into this fracas I will never know; an instinct must have taken over. Step by step, with them holding my hands tightly on both sides, we slowly started moving across the road as all sorts of obstacles sped past and around us, weaving around cars, cows, motorcycles, people. To this day, I don't know how we survived this plunge into madness.

Once we got to the other side, I bent over, trying to catch my breath. The friend departed, kindly offering to meet me the next at morning Aarti on my last day where she'd take me to choose a sacred blanket that had laid for a day on Meher Baba's tomb, a privilege rarely bestowed to visitors at the retreat.

We climbed aboard another rickshaw on a ride that seemed endless through the masses to reach the mercantile part of town. When we came to the row upon row of tall wooden warehouse buildings, my friend pointed out one among many, and as we disembarked, a dark-haired man in a tan Indian outfit emerged,   raising his hand in greeting. As my friend hailed him, he shook her hand and looked very pleased we were there, obviously anticipating great sales. He took out a key to unlock the big grate at the entry of the building. With effort, he pulled the outside panel up to rows upon rows of merchandise within, and I gasped as I saw the tall room with masses of ornate and simple objects in all shapes and sizes! Having already spent most of the funds allocated for the trip, I knew I could only buy the one prized object there, and felt uncomfortable that I couldn't get more, but I was down to my last day!

He took out an enormous ladder and climbed several shelves up against the wall, finally reaching up high to grasp the object, climbing down with it in his hands. We exchanged a barrage of complimentary remarks about it, then, nodding his head, he looked questioningly at me, as if to ask what else did I want? I shook my head, once again embarrassed, my friend trying to explain it was the gloriousness of this one object that was why we had come all this way for it.

After wrapping it in newspaper, he motioned for someone to come forward. A wizened man in a turban all dressed in white appeared and he was pointed towards the package. As I looked at his weathered face, gnarled hands and wrinkled body, he took out one long piece of white string and tightly wrapped the newspaper around the carving and then handed it back.

All the effort and commotion of this day had ended in this one single gesture. Realizing this was his single job to wrap this object, we stood there, silent. Perhaps it was his only job of the day and source of income. The thought that here was a human being with his life based on a piece of white string broke my heart a little. Even though it took the day-long effort to get there and return to the Retreat Center in the continuous rain of the open rickshaw, the old man remained indelible in my mind. I noticed the flimsy quality of the paper money we gave the driver at the end of the ride that could just have melted in the rain, mimicking the insubstantiality of life we'd witnessed. Coming from our heavily endowed Western materialism, I couldn't imagine what invisible threads held together the lives of these people in these countries.

But I knew something profound did in ways perhaps more deeply evocative than the Western ones; ones we not might even be able to imagine. And I think of this man with his gnarled hands and scrawny body like the Fellahin outside the bus at the Hathor Temple in Luxor in Egypt who waved pens at us to buy and take back to the States. His and their memory are eternal to me, not to vanish in the sands of the Sahara or in the teeming masses of India.

28

Last Day in India

Each morning at seven a.m. I'd make the daily pilgrimage to Baba's Samadhi, the white marble tomb where masses of pilgrims came from all over the world to pay tribute.

I'd nod my head silently in greeting to the Indian soldier at the entryway, imagining his nod back was one of spiritual understanding. Always dressed in an immaculately pressed brown uniform and polished shoes, he was impressive in attire so different from the casual pants, long dresses and scarves, jeans and T-shirts that the international devotees wore on retreat.

As I started on the long path to the Samadhi, I would turn to hear a stunning mesmerizing voice of a woman as she chanted the daily Hindu "Bhajan." As if her chants came from high in the sky, her daily calls to prayer were followed by a man's sonorous tones in a lower pitch that summoned Muslim men to the mosques. I always stopped to listen, magnetized by these sounds.

"How could we have lost that evocation of the human voice, calling across distances, so vivid here in their daily call to prayer? Human voices versus silently technological ones?

What has happened to our ability to be stirred by sound in our Western world? In the Southern California, the only constant sound we hear is the rubber of tires from cars on freeways.

The hooded Acacia tree that flung open its wide arms at the walkway's entryway was my next breathtaking stop. Having never seen such an expressive gesticulating tree like that before, it also brought home the startling difference between the Indian subcontinent and the U.S., and reminded me how far away I was from Los Angeles, almost half way around the world.

Green parrots caroused me further down the path in trees that were as vigorously shaped as the Acacia, and because the monsoons had lasted longer that year, I was told the temporary oval-shaped lake below would allow the villagers of ancient Aragaon near the retreat to have more precious water to drink. "What would happen if they didn't have this reprieve? How would they survive?" I wondered as white egrets rested on the wet ground near it, fanning their wings in the heat.

Then on a pathway of white stones, one stepping stone leading to another, I would enter a row of pristine lean trees that marked the entryway towards the Samadhi from the larger path. In meditations since, I have visualized I would pick up a red hibiscus from the ground that would grow to giant proportions once I brought it to the entryway of the Samadhi. There it would be so huge it would cover the entrance, expand over and through the doorway to reach out in huge swirling colors into the sky.

I would also pick a white hibiscus at other times from under the same row of trees, its creamy white color and brilliant red stalk symbolizing the purity of Meher Baba's intention that he had come "not to teach, but to awaken." It would also be alternately placed at the Samadhi's entrance in the same way as the red hibiscus and stream out Baba's intention into the larger world.

Having taken the vow of Silence to emphasize his intention "Not to Teach, but to Awaken," since "when he came before in other incarnations no one listened," he made the commitment not to speak in the last forty-four years of his life. First using an alphabet board, pointing to letters that would make up words the mandali (his male disciples) would translate, he later gesticulated with his fingers and facial expressions that were easy to understand with his animated presence. This vow of silence for the rest of his life was a clear signal to the world and his devotees, that "What is Given and Received in Silence is the most significant transmission of spirit."

On my last day I was honored to choose one of the large cloths that had been created only to lay on the mantle of the tomb for just a day each. Ushered into a small cabin where all the precious materials that had graced the tomb were stacked, I was given just a few minutes to decide which one I would take back permanently to the West as a keepsake, a hard choice, but I knew immediately to select a deep red cloth with light green embroidered flowers intricately sewn upon it. Its strong red vibration drew me, and I carried it carefully in my arms to the site where the crowd was still gathered at the "Aarti." Already packed, my suitcase standing in the hallway of the larger building where I'd meet Patricia and the driver, I held this precious possession in my arms as the group sang "Happy Trails" to me, and tried not to cry.

Now years later I stare at the cloth, and see even more clearly the light filigree of delicate strokes one used to create the chartreuse flowers. They almost float over the surface of the cloth like bulbous discs intricately inscribed onto the material and reflect a richness of color interlaced with devotion and spirit that became a hallmark of my trip.

But the most extraordinary event on this last day was the sudden amazing vision of Meher Baba's hand palm down over the landscape! Like a giant all-encompassing umbrella that not only filled the entire sky and surroundings but covered the ancient village of Aragaon below, it moved further out into the vast distance. Its unexpected sight clarified to me how deeply Baba's inestimable love and protection exists everywhere, and it became particularly evident later that day when surrounded in the teeming streets of Mumbai and the day after in cold dark London.

Back in California, miles away, I am reminded me with irrevocable certainty that Baba exists everywhere in vast silence. Bowled over as I was to witness this sight on my last day there and its connection to the "Spiritual Beloved" in incomprehensible essence, I was thrilled to know it was there and exists for all time.

Blue Mists of the Valley

Dawn has arrived in transparent shades across the sky
As the rat-a-tat of fireworks in the distance
Still celebrate Diwali, the Festival of Lights for Krishna.
Pilgrims on their way to Baba's Samadhi Shrine
Move in a blue mist
Turning to grey blackened by smog and heat
Over the landscape
As the sun, yellow-white in a faint ochre shadow
Starts to succumb to the larger grey clouds,
That becomes a white flaming dot,
Like Meher Baba, a singular white sun,
That guides us all on.
Blue Mists of the Valley
Like Prayers
Rise in the Air,
As the Female Voice
Also like Mist,
Recites Bhajans.
Voices call here across distances
In a way I've never heard before:
The Call to Mystery,
The Call to Prayer.
Kite-shaped green birds
Glide through trees,
Furling their Wings,

And the omnipresent Smokey Voice
Of the Train announces its slithering movement
Through this landscape of mist.
"Beloved Silence,
You Have Swept Me
Into Your Net."

29

Fair LA, My Family's Final Voyage

"Landscape is personal and tribal made visible," wrote
the
geographer Yi-Fu Tuan in his book Space and Place.
"Places are like time machines.
They transport us back to years past."
–Eric Weiner, The Geography of Bliss

Images of my father and aunt in the 1930's dancing at the La Monica Ballroom on the old Santa Monica pier full of glitter and the starry wonder of the Art Deco era; stories of the Hotel Del in Coronado where my newly-engaged parents also danced after cruising over in a small boat, night lights shining in dark waters surrounding them. My father, an ensign out of Annapolis, my mother a new college grad living in Point Loma, their backdrop was a classically beautiful era in stunning landscapes of omnipresent sun and color, a fulfillment of their families' dreams. Later in between our Navy tours the last "classic" memory was swimming in the Coral Casino's huge aqua pool and then plunging into the teeming ocean under luminous Montecito skies.

But my first recollection of Los Angeles while visiting

my aunt in the 1950's was of those quixotic- looking mechanical beings, the yellow oil derricks plunging in and out of the soil, emblematic of the city's promise with its land beckoning of many riches. But also in that land was the dark, viscous morass of oil and water where fleeting bones of leviathans in the La Brea Tar Pits and their connection to the ancient past were overlooked for a more fruitful future.

Grey oozing smog in the 1950's that caused perpetual burning of the eyes and throat was another first story about LA when it was a faraway place from the east coast that none of us dreamt would become a destination years later.

But against all odds, in the 1970's and 80's my family of origin of six with spouses and children reassembled in the L A basin when we could have landed anywhere else in the world, my parents having arrived there from Washington, D.C. in 1971. It was a new golden era we didn't realize we'd share, the last voyage of my family coming together in the culmination of ninety years in the Golden State. A harmonious hospice environment created for my parents' passing eighteen months apart in the late 1990's in Palos Verdes was a fitting ending.

But like so many other families of origin in this country, the group dispersed afterwards to Hawaii, Arizona, Washington State, and the California desert. Living one's life moment by moment in the military, with unexpected change always on the horizon, nine decades of family history was an impressive monument to people and places, memories and time spent together in California.

Looking back, the ride we took "It's a Small Small World," with my aunt on that first visit to LA at the just-opened Disneyland mimicked our small tribe as we sang its words, we then swirling in spinning teacups of the Mad Hat Tea party ride, small pieces of memory bleached into thin air.

Re-arriving as an adult to California in the 1980's, I searched for vestiges of the ancients of LA, wanting to grasp the legacy of the Tongva Indians in the LA Basin and the Chumash who lived up the coast with shells as currency. While these legacies were sadly subsumed by LA's vastness and growing population, there were luckily stronger footprints of other Indian tribes that still existed further east in the California desert, its mountains and valleys. Exploring their legacy were some of my siblings and I happiest times together on camping trips in the 80's and 90's.

However, when my brother, the last of the other sibs to leave informed me in 2011 he was heading for Bainbridge Island overlooking Seattle, Washington after twenty-eight years in LA, I knew I wouldn't be the lone one of this small tribe to stay in the city, and moved out to the mountains and desert.

Where was the continuity of history in our family that had already left so much of its lineage back in Europe, my paternal great- grandparents coming from Norway in 1845 and Prussia in the 1880's to Minnesota? My maternal grandparents' arrival from England was more recent in 1907, Point Loma my grandfather's last stop, and Santa Barbara became the home port address for my family while stationed overseas when my grandmother moved there to be with my aunt. But even now that my cousin, the last of the Santa Barbara tribe has recently passed on, it is no longer a way-station/home either.

"Fair LA, this Last Voyage of my family's history....must I let go of this lineage and start another chapter?" It is a question that has propelled me through new journeys to Glastonbury, Cornwall, Ireland and Scotland, into the sacred stone circles of Avebury and Stonehenge, and also connecting with the earth of New Mexico and waters of Hawaii. It is the sacred in these places and warmth of extended families arising around them that has helped me evolve into a larger world-wide "family." Yet the remnants of the classic California beauty will always remain.

Whenever I return to my favorite beach in Ocean Park, Santa Monica where I've walked so many times since the early 1980's through different chapters of life, I am struck with the image of a future return years later, wondering what more will be revealed? What new stories will emerge from my footsteps and other dear ones on this precious beach, my natural home for years?

Through the lens of new perspectives after so many years, I now know I don't have to let go of the family lineage when starting anew on life's journey. The human psyche's complexity can absorb many threads, interwoven with ninety years of history as a lasting tribute of this family.

A Last Tribute to Los Angeles California

Los Angeles from the top of Griffith Observatory,
The Pacific ocean an arc in the distance
Life by the Golden See...
Where my family planted its seeds for ninety years:
Parents, grandparents, aunts, uncles, cousins,
Siblings, nieces and nephews.
Only to finally remove itself,
The North Star of our heritage
Slowly dimming to a fainter glow.
High above this huge metropolis
In hills holding that magnetism
That originally brought us together,
merged like the viscous tar in the La Brea pits
as sun drenched the new west,
It drew my forebears inextricably on...
But no longer holds our roots.
Now it is just a bright dazzling star,
A life lived briefly by this sea of gold
And I, the last of this small tribe,
Bid it adieu.

30

The Sound of Paper

"You want us to take it now or not, miss?" Two men from the Salvation Army clearing out the split-level home in Los Angeles stood there with my bed on the stairs, the last piece of furniture, ready to take it to the truck.

I watched as they dragged the mattress towards the entryway, its filling cascading down the steps. I had just returned from a nearby garage with news that my car needed another immediate $600 in repairs. It could be worked on in the morning, or I could make a run for it to the mountains in Idyllwild three hours away to a trusted less expensive mechanic. Pausing, I stared at the men. Staying there meant I'd sleep on nothing that night, alone in a big empty house

"Take it!" I shouted, and was soon in wall-to-wall evening traffic heading east on Route 60 out of Los Angeles towards San Jacinto, the car chuntering to a stop and go rhythm all the way.

But when I finally reached that small town two hours later, I knew I'd made it! Half-way to my new life! With large clouds outside the window over a more spacious landscape, I breathed deeply.

Santa Monica, West LA and Palos Verdes in LA had been a home base for almost thirty years, unheard of for someone in a Navy family. So when I arrived at my new place a year later in Palm Springs to teach nearby, I wasn't prepared for the culture shock of the low desert. My body froze at the plethora of gated communities where celebrities' names dwarfed street signs. Friends and family were strewn all over the globe and heat was in the triple digits! What was I doing here?

To handle the shock, I frequented the nearby Rancho Mirage Library as a second office. There I was drawn to the book *The Sound of Paper* by Julia Cameron that I checked out a record six times.

Now, years later, with the faraway view of the Santa Rosa Peaks from my yellow flowered writing desk, I open the book again and read "and so the first act of loving kindness is to start from scratch, the scratch of pen to paper." There I was, the bottom dropped out, "starting from scratch." Back to square one: UCLA employment and the community there no longer, few familiars nearby, and no ocean as my constant companion. "Scratching on paper" was all I could do to bring new life into form.

I had considered moves to England and Hawaii and New Mexico always had its allure. But I had not made the leap. Now a stranger in *this* strange land, it was clear the vines of my psyche had spread much further in Santa Monica than I realized.

Julia nailed it: "We must strive to see the beauty of where

we are planted, even if we are planted somewhere that feels very foreign to our own nature." She intimated that her move from Taos to Manhattan and a friend's similar estrangement into Silicon Valley from Michigan had been challenging, so I tried to emulate this advice by reaching into the hollow spaces of blooming where I was planted.

"Everything is material for a writer" she reminded this friend in Silicon Valley. That made sense. But, the shock continued as I tried to convince myself that being in this sparse desert environment was an opportune time for embracing a new understanding of solitude.

For eons, mystics and revered authors have found solace and salvation in the desert, but even though every year I've basked in its primal spring, I wasn't either. At least wherever I'd settled beloved objects around me had always given me grounding and solace.

"Solitude is one of the most precious things in the human spirit," wrote Irish poet John O'Donohue. "It is different from loneliness. When you are lonely, you become acutely conscious of your own separation. Solitude can be a homecoming to your own deepest belonging." That was what I was now hoping beyond hope to discover.

Haunted by an earlier encounter in a gated community, I watched a handsome woman from LA with dementia placed there by her family while her caretaker and I talked. A well-groomed blond with the straight posture of the advertising professional she once was, she kept turning pages over, one by one, of a lustrous magazine. Seeming to know this was all she could do, this prisoner of poor health ticked away her life with taut strokes of each turning page. Even though her issue was medical, and mine cultural, was she a mirror of my ticking time away in what felt like a sterilized and manicured environment? How would either of us find a way out?

Finally, there was deliverance when Cameron wrote, "If we later decide that we must be transplanted, that our roots are not in soil rich enough for our spirits, at least we have tried, we have kept hold of the initial thread of our being, like the 'I' that gives us the Eye to Behold."

What needed to be written eventually revealed itself. I now knew there was always some truth that needed to be put down on paper, even if it was just, as she described, "a hen's peck in the dirt." Nearby there were areas worthy of exploring—Joshua Tree with its moonscape of a National Park and 29 Palms with its colorful pioneering history. And there were places that still held the resonance of the original Indians' footsteps.

Now, past the half decade time span some say is a measuring stick to adjust to a move and new environment, LA's burgeoning population has begun to swarm out of the city seeking more space in which to live. The openness of the desert has thus become more compelling, and the silence in forests surrounding Idyllwild has always given me a welcome reprieve.

What is the price and what is the gain of new horizons, questions I've now posed in writing workshops I've facilitated:

"What have you lost?"
"What have you gained from those losses?"
"And were those gains worth the losses?"

A pink alpine glow of packed snow hovers over the mountains. Seen from my writing desk, I realize once again how nature has always nurtured me from a young age, and words, like that mist beautifying the mountains have finally flowed into this chapter of my life and onto paper. True, maybe they were "hen's scratches in the dirt," but eventually they did emerge.

Years later, I still overlook the Santa Rosa Mountains from one window, the San Gorgonio and the San Jacinto Mountains from another where dramatic winter storms, winds, and brushes with fire in interminable desert cold and heat have sped by. And finally, in the Pandemic, moving out of the city into more space and safety was a life saver. Sometimes one can only comprehend the rightness of life-changing decisions in hindsight, however long that might take.

On my way to a celebratory gathering with two special women friends in an artist's studio halfway up a stunning corrugated mountainscape, I realized they were the ones I'd been waiting for all these long years, invaluable lifelong companions of the spirit when destiny and time finally intersect.

And if, in the future, the Coachella Valley doesn't have "soil rich enough" for my roots, at least that initial thread of my consciousness has proven to endure, like the 'I' that "gives us the Eye to Behold."

The Way It Is
"There's a thread you follow.
But it doesn't change.
It goes among things that change
People wonder about what you are pursuing.
You have to explain the thread.
But it is hard for others to see.
While you hold it you can't get lost.
Tragedies happen; people get hurt or die,
And you suffer and get old.
Nothing you can do to stop time's unfolding.
You don't ever let go of the thread."
William Stafford

————————➤ *31* ◖————————

Tires at Royal Pines
My First Brush with California Fires

I keep hearing sounds of car doors slamming, tires crunching resolutely in the dirt; hush all around. There weren't any loud noises, just resignation once the evacuation of Idyllwild from the forest fires had been announced in this Royal Pines mobile home park. Perhaps it was to keep from panicking, because even though the fire wasn't at our heels, no licking giant red beast, it felt as if it was still very close, and had been for days.

When I joined the cavalcade of cars beginning that afternoon on Route 74 from the small village in the San Jacinto Mountains to get to Hemet, the town below, everyone seemed to speed up, getting away as fast as they could once they locked their doors and took one last look, perhaps for the last time. That's when panic set in for me, feeling like a refugee out of time and space. I could only assume others felt the same way as we escaped down the winding road together.

I might have been one who witnessed the fire at its very beginning as I drove up the mountain from Hemet two days earlier on Monday afternoon, July 15, at approximately

1:30 p.m. It was then when a plume of white smoke on the right hand side of Tahquitz, Idyllwild's mountain landmark, emerged. Disbelieving, I thought: "Could it really be a fire or just some temporary Illusion?"

Faster and faster I drove up the mountain and it was still there. "It can't really be; it can't really be." My first intimate close brush with any fire in the mountains and forests of California, soon it would become a "new normal," fires constantly igniting because of drought and other conditions brought on by climate change.

But then everything came to a halt at Mountain Center below Idyllwild. I had decided I'd try to outrun it and make it up another thousand feet into town but now no go. In the meantime, I'd called a number of friends saying: "Do you realize there's a fire?" No one had any inkling about it, it was all happening so fast.

Our cars were stopped by police who had no idea how long we'd have to wait to get to Idyllwild. "Two hours maybe." No one knew anything but then we were ordered to vacate as fire engines started to rush through. Just up the hill from us, its source was eventually determined as faulty electrical equipment on private property owned by a Saudi Arabian high government official. Eventually it involved 3500 firefighters, massive amounts of helicopter and plane drops, and was settled for millions of dollars outside of federal court.

As we were ordered out of the scene, motorists looked at each other. "Where do we go?" The only person I talked to was in a large white Cadillac, a tourist from New York, who'd driven the hour and a half all the way from Palm Springs to get a cinnamon bun from Honey Bun's, a local bakery. "If I had only been fifteen minutes earlier," he commiserated as he turned his car around and headed back on Route 74 to the desert.

Suddenly feeling alone, "Who do I call? For what reason?" In the middle of nowhere in between places I could temporarily call home since I'd been camping out with a friend in Royal Pines due to excessive summer heat in the desert, it had become two places.

My escape route was now down two possible routes, 243 to Banning or 74 to Palm Springs. A third choice meant going back to Hemet where I had just been, and then driving all the way around the mountains on Ramona Parkway to 60 east through the Badlands, finally to 10 East to Palm Springs. That would take at least two and a half hours, depending on traffic.

Searing flames were already eating up the land and tall trees nearby next to the mountain, so when told to vacate Mountain Center, I quickly turned the car around to go down Highway 74 towards the desert. No one knew which way the fires would head, but now 74 looked precarious and 243 appeared closed as well. The flames grew larger as the winds mounted, and I knew it was time to leave, feeling odd to be in a collective experience not knowing a soul. Where I'd temporarily stopped my car, people stood unmoving, as if hypnotized by the side of the road watching the fire grow. Some were even taking pictures!

"Time to get out of here!" I turned the car around and shot back down towards Hemet the other way from 74, where I'd finally arrive at Interstate 10. Strange to be at the center of this vortex, watching this enormous amount of unstoppable energy, and then to be so quickly out of it, driving past cars that might have no inkling an emerging fire was happening just a few miles away.

Hours later, finally arriving in Palm Springs, I stopped at Trader Joe's store to another scene of mayhem. People were standing in its parking lot, now staring UP at the mountains, not believing the larger than life red/white/black stack of fire and ashes that was looking like it could sweep right over the mountains to right where we were.

Standing next to me, a woman spoke almost rhapsodically, "Look at that. It's beautiful!" She was completely taken over by its power and energy, unconcerned with any danger. "I was just there," I muttered, "it is a huge fire." She continued to stand in awe, commenting how incredible it looked as it mixed with the red swaths of sunset while I imagined Idyllwild at risk.

A radio announcer in the car reported, "Yes, there's a fire near Idyllwild, but it's not a problem and won't go past 111 in Palm Springs." It seemed I couldn't get away from this inferno as I was now right on 111, apart from but included in another surreal scenario.

Two days later the fire appeared to be heading directly for Palm Springs and maybe even Palm Desert, so there was less concern for Idyllwild, but just in case, I decided to move everything from the mobile home where I'd been staying.

And lo and behold: Wednesday, as I was back in the town getting my possessions, the winds and fires started their errant return that way, and the evacuation was announced for all to leave Idyllwild. It took three long days afterward before we could return to Idyllwild after staying with friends in Hemet. The fires were finally quashed even though they were still smoking and sparking for days after in the mountains above Palm Springs.

One last memory: in the parking lot near the Idyllwild Post Office, at high noon that Wednesday right before the evacuation was announced, a group had gathered to watch a red King Kong-like plume rear itself, trying to come over the South Ridge. "That makes me nervous," a usually calm friend said. There was an ominous silence as everyone just stared at what could be the end of the town if the fire bested that ridge which it tried to do several times.

Postscript: two weeks later, after an emotional tribute to firemen, state and national park rangers and other officials instrumental in stopping the fires had been given a long standing ovation by townspeople as they stood on the stage of the Idyllwild Summer Concerts, popular jazz musician Sherry Williams proclaimed over the mike :

"Welcome home, Idyllwild. Your home is still standing."

Tears rolled down faces as the community applauded and cheered again and again and then she started singing, they danced!

32

There are Many Different Roads to the Oasis in Twenty-Nine Palms

There are many roads that lead to the Oasis in Twenty-Nine Palms, California. One is by the low road with its tales of survival of those who traversed the land for sustenance of food and water. With their earliest migratory footsteps across vast desolation, the Oasis of Mara was their first glimmer of hope. Not only did it replenish them, its rich soil was the foundation for seeds and plants for centuries.

Flying across the desert with its mists of wind, sand, and rugged buttes below, I've always been struck by its inescapably barren territory. The green of the Colorado River seems minute in comparison to this unceasing Colorado desert and one wonders how it allowed anyone to survive. How did these migratory people manage to walk such long distances over hundreds of miles from one bit of water to the next?

The second inspiring road to 29 Palms proceeds down 2000 feet from popular Skull Rock in the Park towards its Northern entrance. After sunset a purple glow swirls over the earth making the timeless landscape into a painting of vast distance.

And then there is the high road of history. With the desert's clear dry air bringing many ailing from respiratory diseases or having been gassed in World War I, they not only regained their health but flourished and this elation translated into building a most unusual community. And years earlier the white man arrived who made their mark upon the land when surveyors, miners, cowboys, and cattlemen came searching for gold and lusting for whatever the Wild West could offer. It remains today reflected in murals created by artists on walls throughout town.

And finally there is the more comforting road of Spirit for those who needed the contemplation and reflection this land affords them. Whether they are rock climbers challenging their prowess on cliff-hanging boulders in the Park, or those reveling in the psychological view space so critical to balance their lives in teeming masses of population just over the hill, this land has provided a necessary sanctuary from past centuries to recent days.

* * *

42 Palms to 29 Palms

When one passes the "Whitewater" junction on Interstate 10 going east, usually speeding 70-80 miles an hour below pointed San Jacinto mountain peaks, it's hard to believe that a mere seventy years ago no road existed from there through the Morongo Basin to 29 Palms. Whitewater was the end of the road. It was the last mail stop to "29."

Now bevies of windmill towers lurch like misshapen star machines under the sky on bold freeways, entryways to nearby Palm Springs in the low desert. But less than a hundred years ago, travelers made arduous tracks on sandy dirt on horses, burros or wagons for trips that lasted days to get to this destination. In the first motor cars, on one lane by-ways heading through gorges and mountains, if two vehicles came in opposite directions, one had to pull off the track to let the other past.

Imagine as you begin to travel up the first grade into Morongo Basin the massive earth movements of such Herculean proportion thousands of years ago that created this separate corridor of mountainous valleys, streams, and landscape where there was only solid rock before. Now cars overcome those sheer heights of the two steep grades into Yucca Valley in record minutes, and it is dizzying to think how quickly this special "spur" between the Colorado and Mojave deserts has transformed.

Those lucky enough to be settling into camping areas at night in the Park can look forward to a primal black night filled with thousands of stars. If they approach by nightfall, they might pass by furry silver silhouettes of cholla cactus, or by day green pencil cactus needles glistening gold in the sun or white bulbs of waving creosote brush by the side of the road.

It was on that long tract down Utah Trail that makes a

left-hand turn into Park Headquarters and the Oasis Visitor's Center where my family first arrived in the early 1980's. I can't remember the moment of first sight, but I did know in that instant that this town of 29 Palms in the High Desert with its precious oasis would be imprinted on my being for years to come.

33

The Green Dream

A year later after this re-immersion into 29 Palms in 2013, I was commissioned to write a manuscript for a well known pioneering family in California with its final result a possible coffee table book.

However, as writers with large projects can experience, I was whacked with anxiety. Commissioned for this six month project by Janie Smith, of 29 Palms Inn, the Granddaughter of the patriarch who purchased and built upon the family's desert properties, she had used few words for direction. "Surprise me!" she said.

In the early months, at a house near the Inn I had been given to write in, I'd been pulling my hair out for the most appropriate way to enter the material. Should it be tales of pioneers and grizzly bears chewing the ears off of those of explorers who first came to California? About wagon trains, miners and cowboy outlaws who once lived in this trackless area? These hugely popular stories had already been written about several times and the project was intended to be a story of this family's contributions, connection to the land, and stewardship of the only privately-owned sacred site of the Oasis of

Mara in Southern California.

Having completed two years of research about the family and hearing their history over the years I stared endlessly at a particular wall of the house, imploring the muse to come through. Surrounded by masses of notes, I couldn't figure out how to put the pieces of this puzzle together. In my mind's eye, I kept seeing a stagecoach blasting through the wall that would miraculously direct me towards writing the history of this pioneering family that would satisfy all. But then I would see old black type on dusty pages in books that had already lingered on shelves for far too long. I knew something new and vibrant had to be created that would be an original way to encapsulate this family and their link to the land they had successfully nurtured since 1918.

As I watched myself procrastinate in the early months of this project, conversing with old geezer writers at the local restaurant, hanging out with others to talk endlessly about any other subject but this one, I knew the clock was ticking. My stomach was in knots. Even though I had already authored poetry and non-fiction books, the only other challenge I had faced like this was when the publisher in England needed me to finish *Bringing the Soul Back Home: Writing in the New Consciousness*, in six months when I had then sustained a broken wrist in Hawaii.

Like a dog circling its tail, I would sit and stare at the wall. I'd wrestle with rough draft chapters when not at the kitchen writing table with a wobbly leg that had been pulled over to

French doors looking out on the vast desert. There I would be absorbed in the large Mesquite bush right in front that housed a little universe of migrating desert finches, a Gamble quail family and albino iguanas.

Waiting, waiting, waiting.... I assembled albums from boxes of historical and family photographs earmarked for the book that were supposed to eventually accompany the writing. But that wasn't the task at hand.

Then, finally, one night, as panic increased, in the 11th hour, the "Green Dream" came through:

"Make the Center of the Book Green"
"What?"
"Make the Center of the Book Green."

And yes, it was coincidentally right around St. Patrick's Day, the mythical bringing in the green!

Then I knew what I had to do. The large encompassing garden on the property with its rich soil that had come endlessly from waters of the Oasis, feeding it for centuries, was the central theme of the book. The life that had been abundant there symbolized the family's long-term commitment and one could see this connection in the photographs of the patron's father as he stood under sprawling sunflowers in the Victory Garden he'd created in the 1940's.

He looks proudly in contemplation over the garden that he loved with deep regard, and eventually this writing project was dedicated to him.

When I awakened from the dream the next morning,

I knew this was the right direction: embracing the family's accomplishments while also celebrating the earth and waters that made the area so fertile in food and wildlife that villages had arisen and thrived from in past centuries. The energy of these indigenous peoples still existed in the space. And to this day the Oasis remains the unspoken heart center of the town surrounding the land, where residents bring babies and graduating seniors and all others to be photographed on ceremonial occasions. Weddings are held there as well and many other community events and arts festivals.

"Bingo!" I could now proceed. The "Green Dream" provided the axis around which the material and direction could spin, the focus being interviews with family members through their own eyes to capture the family's challenges and triumphs over the years. Beginning with the early history through words of the grandfathers, fathers and mothers who had passed on, the book would then include stories from the patron and her siblings, turning finally to the impassioned younger generation who now claimed their commitment to the family enduring on this land and continuing to make it prosper.

Capturing the special quality of the garden and its history, I also interviewed the head gardener about her impressions of its lasting significance for her and the guests who walked through its rows of vegetables, herbs and plants, enjoying its produce in the Inn's restaurant.

Yes, the "Green Dream" had captured this significance of a garden with soil continuously enriched by waters of the

Oasis, and what a relief was to discover the link for all the other stories of this family's contributions that would also include its special guardianship of this sacred site.

My lesson? "Believe in the Dream!"

How had I been able to do this?

Years earlier I had had another pivotal dream during a similar cliff-hanging creative experience with a deadline when I was the curator of an art exhibition at the State Capitol in Sacramento. There art work was placed outside of the Governor's office and first floor hallway to an enthusiastic opening crowd. But it had been another challenge to bring this about.

As curator of arts exhibitions before I turned to full-time writing, I was given the opportunity when I worked at UCLA Extension to assemble with staff from two other statewide arts organizations the remarkable art from California prisons. This triad of arts organizations from Northern to Southern California had sponsored art classes over a period of time in the prisons and wanted to demonstrate the dexterity and craftsmanship of the art that had come from the classes to the public.

Enlisting the aid of fellow students at the graduate USC Museum Studies program to help install the approximately one hundred multi-media pieces, and with help of staff from these other organizations, it seemed we were in good shape to create the exhibition in a short period of time. Or so it had seemed until, upon arrival in Sacramento, there was little remaining budget for the installation of the art work.

There we were, a small volunteer group, sweating in summer weather in the dark hallways of the Capitol building where the art work had originally been relegated to three floors above its entrance with little lighting for the exhibition. The staff of the Capitol couldn't be convinced that proper lighting or the right equipment was needed to install it. Then the deadline for the exhibition was looming nearer and nearer and anxiety escalated.

One night, as in the "Green Dream," I got the message while asleep:

"Water the art work."

That seemed like the craziest advice a dream could ever give. Waking up, I realized: What do plants need other than water? Light! And what does art need, because like plants, it has a vitality that gives similar inspiration. Both need water and light to survive, and like an organic substance, art has to have the proper light.

The next morning our team moved the art, piece by piece, to the more naturally lit ground floor outside the Governor's office, placing it throughout the area where there was appropriate natural lighting. It was now in its proper place, and the exhibition opening on time was enthusiastically received by the prisoners' families, politicians, residents of Sacramento and staffs from surrounding government offices and arts organizations.

A thank you card I received from the wife of Juan Carrillo, a minimum security prisoner, was particularly moving. Juan had used his imagination to fashion the pits of nuts and fruits into miniature Japanese-like monkeys and other animals. His craftsmanship and special eye for his subject was among the most popular of the art work, and his wife thanked me for bringing it to public exposure because it was the love his life.

In retrospect, both dreams had pulled me through these challenging professional experiences, and assisted me twice to find creative solutions that brought about successful outcomes and so I will always remember the power of "The Green Dream."

A Postscript:

While leading a tour of women writers to sacred sites in Avebury in Southwest England in summer, 2015, I had a reunion with the owner of the illustrious Henge Shop in the center of the tiny village of standing stones of Avebury. Belgian Philippe Ullens was not only an art collector and preserver of sacred sites, but an extraordinary photographer of beauty in all its glowing forms around the world. His book of photography, Crop Circles, Beauty and Soul, *records in chronological order the impressive crop circle creations that have emerged in the summers around Avebury since 2000. While we talked by one of the massive stones in the field, he pointed out that my "writing mission" has been to record sacred sites around the world, as I had done at the Oasis and garden in the desert with its "Green Dream, " at the stones of Avebury, and in Yellowstone National Park where I had been a writer-in-residence.*

In this book on crop circles there is a description of the meaning of the Color Green I found particularly significant when remembering the "Green Dream":

Speaker: *"....the Energy of Nature is one of Creation. And Love is the energy of Creation, therefore they are one and the same."*

Questioner: *"Is it significant that our plants and trees are green?"*

Speaker: *"The energy of the Heart is Green...the Heart Energy is Green. Other colors may come and go but it will always remain in that state of balance and love.* **Green is the Color of Love.***"*

34

Perseid Meteor Showers and Scorpions

Coming down the San Jacinto mountain at my first invitation from Janie Smith (who would eventually commission me to do a book on the Legacy of her family in 29 Palms, California), I'd just left the enclosed pine and cedar forests of Idyllwild at 5000 feet. But how was I to know I would be entering another exciting chapter and terrain in my life?

Even though I'd been looking forward to this trip to learn more about the wilderness that still existed in the High Desert, I paused at the Whitewater Rest stop off the 10 Freeway heading east towards Route 62.

Concerned about the recent rains pulverizing the desert, I called over to 29 Palms Inn on the telephone: "Janie, they say the road is closed because it's flooded there."

"Oh no, you'll be fine," she reassured me, "We get floods here all the time. This time the road is closed after the Inn. So come on down."

Excited to be on a new trail exploring the culture and history of the area, I was in good timing. A year later, the area exploded with national and international tourists when

Joshua Tree Monument became a National Park, and the Inn with its own lively history was right at its footsteps. It also was the site of the only privately owned Oasis of Mara in Southern California. That year when I arrived, it still felt like a rarefied place hidden away and kept, almost deliberately, as a secret treasure.

After another huge storm happened while I was there, Janie, barefoot, exclaimed, "Let's jump in the car and see what has happened to the property!" We spun out over dirt roads seeking new adventure as we laughed our heads off.

That summer was memorable for another reason. Viewing for the first time on a larger stage the annual August Perseid meteor showers , I watched them fill the skies from a battered chaise lounge in the back yard of the Old Dale House (named after the Old Dale Mine). In the still warm desert air around 2:30 a.m., they pushed over and over again through countless levels of stars and the white mists of the Milky Way, new constellations seeming to appear within the showers every minute. Witnessing this eternal reality in rapture just beyond earthly comprehension, I was thrilled to be part of this cosmological event night after night.

But it was on that first night that a moment that often surfaces in my mind struck me when I walked out of the darkness back into the rustic kitchen of the Old Dale. As I turned on a light in a closet, I was surprised by the tiniest of scorpions that waved its pink shrimp-like limbs at me, seeming to scream: "Turn it off! Turn it off! That light is too bright.

Please turn it off!" Coming from such universal vastness to this smallest little constellation, my heart suddenly stopped. I knew instantly we shared a deep communion as two creatures trying to make our fragile way on this complex earthly journey.

I gently scooped it up in a broom pan and placed its delicate body somewhere outside the kitchen door, back to its terrain in the dark glittering panoply of stars. To this day I am still touched when I think of it and the mutual vulnerability that we share amplified that night by those giant starry skies. Whether or not I ever encounter another one quite like it, that little pink scorpion will always remain in my consciousness and heart.

35

My Grandmother's Gift

*"It is faith that steers us through stormy seas,
faith that moves mountains
and faith that jumps across the ocean."
(Mahatma Gandhi)*

Dilys said: "Your mother wants you to ask your sister about the Marcasite brooch."

I'd known I had to see Dilys again when I arrived back in England in 2015. Eleven years before this spiritual intuitive had surprised me in a reading when she connected me with my father, a most healing experience. Now there were more surprises. I hadn't been in touch with my mother for seventeen years since she'd passed on, but here I was leading another tour of women writers to Glastonbury, UK, and here she was speaking about a brooch I had no idea even existed.

A second surprise in that reading was that my grandmother also needed to speak to me. Sharing only rare moments with her since my family travelled from one place to another in the Navy, she remembered we bonded while she rocked me to sleep in Santa Barbara while my mother took care of my older twin brother and sister, my father at sea. She confirmed we have a long standing connection still alive today.

For instance, when we were both sixty, years apart in time and geography, we'd both broken our shoulders in the exact same place. "And you have the same laugh!" Dily said. One never knows who will show up in these readings with their urgent messages like this, but they are always at the right time and beneficial.

"The English maternal side of the family is still a vital living force for you," my grandmother said. My grandparents had arrived in 1907 from England and family stories passed on from there were deeply etched in my psyche. I'd gone as a young adult back in 1985 where I had an extraordinary experience with a stone in the Avebury Stone Circle that became the subject of a book, and have visited often since 1997 where two other books were fostered.

Returning to Yorkshire in 1998 to take my mother's ashes to her favorite childhood spot where her family visited in the 1920's, I became close to the next generation of the McKell's, Harry and Daphne while leading women writers on pilgrimages to sacred sites there since 2000,

But a Marcasite brooch? And why had it now suddenly appeared?

Could it be some missing piece in the puzzle that my grandmother urgently needed to tell me: "that I was not alone," a whole ancestral family surrounded and supported me that it represented? She must have given it to my mother after my grandfather gave it to her, possibly even as a wedding present? And then it went to my sister when my mother passed. But my sister didn't even remember it until searching for it high and low in her belongings in Hawaii.

When I finally did receive it from Hawaii in the next Christmas package, it felt I'd been given a talisman that had travelled over centuries in ancient times and places. Stunned by its elegance, it immediately brought back additional stories of both grandparents' families, the only one of my siblings who has ever travelled back to England and listened to these myths.

Jewelers surmised it was white topaz surrounded by an elaborate design of silver Marcasite when Queen Victoria made it fashionable. Now in my hands, it had a once-in-a-life-time significance. Strangers still come up to me when they see it, asking what it is and where from, often just staring at it. White topaz raises vibration, enhances spiritual abilities and awareness, purifying and clearing a body's energy.

The only member of her family of six siblings who left her homeland in Yorkshire, England to come to America, what was my grandmother thinking on those days during that oceanic passage alone with one trunk that represented her life and belongings? I imagine her standing outside on the deck of the ship, waves crashing below, thinking of the family and home she had left to start this new life in a faraway place. She would be meeting her soon-to-be husband from Yorkshire waiting at the Boston docks and only returned a few times with him and two daughters as children. During World War II, when the Japanese were possibly going to fire upon California, her relatives begged her to come back to England. "Mary, you're in danger!" they'd exclaimed, under more threat than she.

As a young courting couple they walked miles across the moors of Yorkshire to be together, she from the small town of Gargrave with its church tower built in the 1400's, he from the market town of Skipton. Walking the land was a part of life in those days, and in that green vastness, they agreed to start a new life in America together. I imagine my grandfather, who I never met, was the one with the larger desire to travel, to see the world, especially away from the rigid class-conscious English society.

But it was still my grandmother who had to board that ship alone, knowing her whole life would change. They would be married in the famous Trinity Episcopal Church on Copley Square in Boston and I was touched by the story that John McKell, Mary Elizabeth's father and other bellringers at St. Andrews Church rang the bells thousands of miles away at the time of their marriage.

They moved from St. Louis, Missouri where my mother and aunt were born to Sao Paolo, Brazil, where my grandfather continued his career as a Chartered Public Accountant of Price-Waterhouse, the ticket to more overseas travel. Photographs of their exotic three-storied house in a jungle-like landscape show a startling contrast to Yorkshire. Then they returned to Evanston, Illinois before moving to California, their final destination, and spent time travelling all over the West, especially to national parks, like Banff and Lake Louise in Canada. Pictures show shining eyes, the girls loving those adventures, driving in an open air motor car on dirt roads.

Once my grandmother told me, "Remember we come from Beauty." Both her daughters spent their lives surrounded in it, my mother in Monterey, Hawaii, Paris, on the rolling countryside of Virginia outside of Washington, D.C., and finally overlooking views of the Pacific Ocean in California, my aunt in the resplendent historic city of Santa Barbara. In keeping with the traditional English love of roses, both also created large rose gardens as my grandfather had in Point Loma where they settled before Santa Barbara. It is Ironic that my grandfather passed on at the early age of 58 that was due to supposedly being pierced by a thorn from his rose garden. Having travelled so far, my grandmother then lived the rest of her life in Santa Barbara near her daughter and family.

Dilys explained that the word "Death" was originally the French word "De-ath" and pronounced that way in French giving it a whole different vibration when spoken in English. She continued, "They are always there to help when help is needed, and give us guidance too. If one thinks of their loved ones as dead, not existing anymore, it is doubly hard for them to reach us. They want you to know they encircle you with care and are fully present with their love for you."

When she said this, I suddenly saw my nuclear family in a small circle of light with love around me encircled by larger and larger circles of each generation of ancestors moving on endlessly through time and space. In this world's condition, it is a promising message to have. Lessons of surviving the unknown come from ancestors who didn't know the outcome but risked a new path anyway. My grandmother's model to face this unknown with her passing on the Marcasite brooch helps us to understand this wisdom for future generations.

And as the topaz glistens today brilliantly etched by the Marcasite around it, its ancient wisdom and the words of Dilys, "you are never alone," reaches out to us all. Perhaps that is why it appeared at this time. Thank you, Grammy, from the bottom of my heart.

36

My Sojourn at the Hospital

I am standing in a green and black flecked hospital gown that has strange pockets everywhere and squiggly black designs all over it. I am oddly in two gowns at once, one tied forward, the other backward to accommodate wires I will carry or that will be attached to me.

Those who brought me from the Emergency Room seem to have vanished, and all of a sudden, I find myself looking out from this hallway at Eisenhower Hospital through what appears to be an illusionary window into a greater vision. Through my confusion come the sudden words: "It Doesn't Matter!"

"It just doesn't matter. It never has!!"

Shocked that I am here at all, the first time in a hospital since eight years old for a tonsillectomy, these words blow through my whole system and breathe a critical message I probably could only have received at this stage in my life.

I suddenly understand in graphic terms : "All the times I tried so hard from childhood to adulthood to be "enough," were never that important! Nor has approval from others, to be 'all right' in their and my eyes—it just wasn't ever that important. My purpose in life has meant so much more than that. All that time and effort wasted!!!

Do I get it? "It doesn't matter. It never has." Where this information was coming from I couldn't follow, just that it came like a blinding light.

Unexpectedly here from the ER after abnormal lab tests I'd had in Urgent Care on Friday with the follow-up call at 8 a.m. this early Sunday morning.

"You need to come to the hospital right away!" I thought it must be another case of dehydration from living in the desert that had brought me to the same ER some years back. I tried to stay calm when I got in the car. Getting gas seemed to help, though after it was purchased, I forgot to pump it in and drove away.

When I turned into the corner where the red Emergency Room Sign pointed at Bob Hope Drive, a place I'd never thought I'd have to go again, I felt oddly astray. The emergency room at that hour was empty and I was soon ushered in for a range of tests.

And now, as I stood in this hallway of sorts in the beginning of my seventh decade of life, this critical message pressed more deeply into my skin:

"It just doesn't matter! Let it go!": the overwhelming need for the ego to be "ok" since childhood jettisoned for a more existential truth.

Then I was ushered by nurses into what could have been a luxury hotel to a clean and sparkling corner room with no other patients and big windows. Large vases of suffused glass in subdued colors in artistically-lit alcoves down the hall completed the picture of this pristine formal space. Where was I and what was I doing here? After more tests and CT Scans in the emergency room, the nurse there had stated in a matter of fact way: "You're going upstairs" as my mouth dropped, "You're sending me *up*???" I exclaimed. "Where am I going and why?" I had thought my fever was from an infected tooth I was going to have taken out, but when the dentist finally said after waiting for some time he wouldn't work on it with my feverish conditions, I had scooted immediately over to Urgent Care.

Was all this about an important lesson that I had been brought here to learn? Even though the obvious reason was a high fever from an infection I didn't understand I had, it seemed I was also standing at a significant portal of awareness.

Waiting for the fever to go down and the infection to abate in the next three days, hooked to machinery and intravenous tubes, constant blood tests all hours of the day, I was in a circus of attention. There was a constant stream of nurses and an entourage of doctors of different specializations. Because it was a residential teaching hospital, teams of residents guided by their leaders came to study my condition. And finally there was a Chinese surgeon who pronounced that I had diverticulitis that luckily had not invaded my stomach wall, even though he continued to watch the situation closely.

A volunteer minister also stopped by who wanted to know what religion I was and if I wanted to pray. Instead, we embarked on a long discussion of philosophy and mortality until he finally had to go, followed by a friendly volunteer with newspapers. "Did I want one?" I pointed to a coloring book with crayons, and he smiled rather gleefully.

In this surreal time out of time, with my normal life disengaged completely, friends called and if I could reach the phone, we'd speak. One friend I will never forget became a constant daily companion. When I realized this stay was more serious than I understood, I quickly called Reiki friends and asked all sorts of healers to do absent healing from afar. Meanwhile, the initial lingering ghost of truth that had come to me in the hallway never left me.

During the day, and all day, I would be moved to tears while watching the Nature Channel on the television in the room. On it were ongoing pictures of all sorts of animals who seemed to come close to the edge of the screen with penetrating eyes and noses. "We are a profound part of your life on earth, but where have you been?" they seemed to say. "Why haven't you spent more time closer to the earth and to us?"

Other constantly rotating images on this channel portrayed lush landscapes with small and large flowers, many with water pouring down in a variety of cascading waterfalls and fountains. I was beginning to sense these visual images were like messages about what had been significantly missing from my life. Have our birthright as humans living close to nature been replaced by living in more urban settings, to become solely devoted to the information age and its technology with computers, cell phones, and massive changes in communication?

This train of thought was underscored by nighttime viewing on this same "Care" channel of earlier animals and landscapes. Now brilliant images of purple, blue and pink galaxies composed of perpetual stars and elliptical sliding light repeated over and over again, mystical music in the background. Shimmering golden slides of light slithered across the screen in gauzy motion, portraying the infinite eternal space of this cosmos, and a certain luminous planet of gold dissolved and re-formed as it came close to the edge of the screen.

Spellbound by these images, they helped me understand how precious it is to be part of this galaxy at this time and to share it together with others who are here on earth as well. Reinforcing how particularly significant is this present we inhabit on this golden slide of light, which other dear ones have already left, this experience gave me the gift I'll never forget about the ephemeral beauty of existence and the altar created by those we know here and now in the present.

Another thudding realization came later on this speedway of mortality. Along with the veils of the ego lifting, I began to see I was "not invincible," for never before this moment had I realized how much I'd convinced myself I was. Now I wondered how it is that humans con ourselves into believing this. Was it a way to keep our survival mechanism going? When the human shell shows itself as impermanent, and drops away, we are shocked. What we thought was invincible, that would carry us through anything, isn't true. And yet somehow this new awareness can make one stronger and we can feel relief that we don't have to always be invincible.

Months before, I had launched my fifth book under huge pressure. After leading a sacred site tour for women writers to Ireland in August, 2017 as the first leg of the trip that included many challenges, I travelled to Glastonbury, England to present my new book *Awakening in Avebury: A Woman's Call to Pilgrimage*. Portraying my experiences in the largest stone circle in England, Avebury, the book's production involved numerous last minute decisions before leaving for Ireland. In a short amount of time, I mounted a previously unexpected fund raising campaign, and finished last minute proofreading and consultations with the Glastonbury designer and printing company in England. Even determining the book's ISBN number that should have been simple seemed a daunting task.

Sitting on the shelf a long time since my other books had to be published before this one, its arrival was particularly significant. The tremendous relief that came with birthing it in England was followed with no letting up upon my return to California, starting classes in writing at universities, doing other book signings, and leading weekend writing retreats for women. Short weeks later, I was in the hospital.

Now alone in this simulated luxury hotel a.k.a. Eisenhower Hospital in Rancho Mirage, California, sick as a dog and not having realized it, I contemplated the extraordinary lessons that might have only caught my attention on just this kind of a sojourn in this hospital. The pallid sterility of white buildings surrounded by ever present palm trees I had been staring at out the window underscored those taut messages.

"You are not Invincible, and it's ok."

These benign messages were clear. We truly can Let Go!! "We are all born just fine, not in need of anyone else's or our own approval, for that matter. We are loved and have always been loved."

As they wheeled me out of the hospital homeward bound through a now densely over-crowded emergency room, I vowed to re-enter my life gratefully, trying to live a more normal, less pressured life. The overriding task has been to incorporate this new wisdom and to pace myself with this understanding. Trying to remember to slow down, breathe, and let go of internalized pressure and stress, the memorable words "It really doesn't matter, and that "It is all OK!" have become a lifelong credo for me.

I just hope I can remember and follow them throughout the next years of my life, when as Mother Julian of Norwich once wrote:

"All Shall Be Well,
And All Shall Be Well,
And All Manner of Thing
Shall Be Well."

37

Tsunami Warnings In LA?

Tsunami warnings in LA marking the new year 2022? A volcano erupts underwater near Tonga and suddenly the whole West Coast of the United States is on alert? It reminds me of the other giant tsunami that washed out the continents of southern India, Thailand and Myanmar in 2004 and when I was on a puddle jumper to Australia from Los Angeles between jobs in 1988. There other passengers and I were disembarking on one of our many stops at two a.m. in Fiji.

This is when I had my first encounter with the island of Tonga. I was bewildered when we got off the plane why slight men, on guard, seemed nervous holding machine guns as they stared at everyone passing by, even those from our plane?

I got myself to a refreshment stand for coffee, and at that moment a most unusual entourage of Pacific Islanders moved slowly by. Following a remarkable man, the King, in a resplendent outfit of golds and brocades in a large skirt, green silken shirt, with wooden leis around his neck, his feet were in bejewelled sandals. He walked with a regal bearing, as he led his subjects, their heads down as they promenaded by

"I want to go there, wherever they're going! I want to go there!" I surprised myself. Sensing they were on their way somewhere to a completely different world beyond my imagination, I was caught in the whirlpool thought that my life could change in an instant. I then saw they were heading to the gate for Tonga into the darkness of the Pacific Ocean, mother of all mother oceans. Later I was to learn that Tonga had so many islands in that immense space that sometimes they weren't even named. And in that vastness the volcano had erupted?

"What was going on in Fiji?" I questioned my friend when I arrived hours later in Sydney, but she didn't respond. A week later, she mentioned, "oh yeah, they just had a coup!" Well, I have never forgotten Fiji or the King of Tonga.

"Tsunami," the word evokes images of powerful destruction. Remembering the one that smashed into three continents in 2004, I was also taken back to that December when I was in Heathrow Airport on my way to Los Angeles for Christmas. Before take-off I'd walked down a corridor where there were signs directing passengers to Thailand and I watched the holiday travelers moving towards that gate.

"What would it be like to go to Thailand right now?" I mused again transfixed by the idea of changing course in midstream in my travels. "Who are those people sliding suitcases behind them and what awaits them?"

Later, I heard the story of how the first radio operator, a young man in the vast Pacific, had received word of a possible tsunami, but because it seemed too impossible of a reality, he didn't notify authorities in time. Is he still haunted by this decision two decades later?

A friend there teaching scuba diving at that time said if it hadn't been for the elephants who felt the impending disaster before anyone else, many lives were saved by their startled reactions as they headed for the nearby hills. This friend lived right at the beach, and was saved with her partner by jumping on a motorcycle heading up steep hills to higher ground just in time. The amazing coincidence is that the only thing left in their place when they returned was a musical instrument found in a closet.

But on this particular trip to Australia, where we went to tourist spots in Sydney, the bush and mountains of New South Wales, held wombats in our arms at nature parks and side stepped kangaroos on sidewalks, I was to learn there are other kinds of tsunamis, personal ones, that can also wreak havoc in your life. In one of my last days there, I was alone on a train heading to tour the white scalloped Opera House in Sydney. And suddenly, just as we crossed a bridge over its great harbor, I felt a lurch in my stomach I knew immediately instinctively with the shock of absolute knowledge I was unexpectedly pregnant. How could this be? And how could this happen on the other side of the world from home in a place where I was more alone and vulnerable than I'd ever been in my life before.

My friend, her daughters and I had hiked days before in the bush outside of Sydney, and came upon a small museum in a park. Through the clouded window of the closed building, there were opaque jars containing strangely shaped small beings on display, and as we got closer we realized they were actually embryos of tiny animals. Suddenly nauseous, I turned quickly away. "My body knew what my mind didn't want to know" flushed through me on the train in shock.

It was a miscarriage when I returned to LA,, and in the post-hormonal gloom, it seemed to last a long time. In my new job at the City of Manhattan Beach, I would stare at the dark Pacific waters after work, and often remark to myself how my gloom matched that darkness and how it came upon me so far from home. Yet I survived it.

Be it a global or personal tsunami, one finally understands these experiences are the building blocks of our lives , whether we are suddenly witness to an unexpected coup, a regal king's entourage, startling life changes or washes of huge waters over continents.

38

Wonder Valley Writes
The Full Moon in Scorpio

As I watched the full moon last night, a yellow orb the only object in the sky covering a distance of forty miles over Wonder Valley, I remembered its appearance years ago! Running out to see it at the same time of year in 2012 as its huge globe just came over the Joshua Tree Mountains, I was stunned by its enormity. Then only a rounded half moon, it dwarfed the mountains' curves as it rose behind them.

Returning to where I was staying, I was soon compelled to see it again, and jumped back in the car to drive into Joshua Tree National Park through the west entrance. As I stopped by the side of the road to watch it rise, cars moving slowly behind me in the dark, it grew larger and larger. It was the time this book of essays was being born and I marveled at its huge sight over the sinuous outcroppings of mountains

That next morning I was at the two tiered black desk, its sheen seeming to glisten, in a self-made writing retreat for seven weeks. Finally back with the writing, where I could concentrate on it like I hadn't been able to for some time, it was similar to the "ah ha" moments of focus at my writer-in-residencies at Yellowstone National Park and when enrolled in

Antioch's MFA Creative Writing Program. Each time, living on a self-imposed edge, I allowed myself to be with the muse no matter what would come, if anything. Alone in silent companionship with the words, images abounded.

With red, green and yellow notebooks, I decided each one would represent a theme or chapter in my life to write about. Looking both forward and backward, I suddenly felt I was in a race with time, as if it were running out as never before. Then five years until a new decade, I pondered: "What will I write? How will I convey what my life has meant up to now? I won't be here again, and living at this time on Earth with its challenges and inspirations, what does taking certain paths marking this journey mean and how will that be useful to others?"

Now as I walk down the road this morning towards Pinto Mountain in Wonder Valley outside Joshua Tree, bare zigzagging tracks up and down across it, I feel calmer to be near land still in wildness. With the last road sign I'd passed before reaching Coyote Casita announcing "100 miles to the next services," I felt the essence that nearby 29 Palms in the 1920's and 1930's once had. That was when the first homesteaders arrived after being gassed in World War I, uncertain they would survive. Since its air was the purest in the Southwest, as determined by medical authorities, these pioneers decided to make a go of it, and surprised everyone, including themselves, when they stuck it out and labored to make a prosperous town.

Naturalists have written that there have to be more spaces on earth where the human imprint has never existed or at least does not dominate. And now, on this road today seeing the pioneers' abandoned homestead cabins scattered across the terrain where nature still has the bigger impact, it is a relief to be here.

Under last night's full moon, like the same Scorpio moon that appeared years ago, I thought about the past years I've spent writing these essays, imagining it would take much less time to finish them. Trying to fill those multi-colored note-books in the desert's isolation in that 2012 retreat and later at another desk in Palm Springs, I often wondered why I was writing these essays hearing they wouldn't make any differ-ence, or be of interest, or so the critic said. But still they had to be done.

Now I realize that perhaps I wrote them with that same living on the edge conviction the pioneering homesteaders had when they came to 29. Going deep into the earth to find water to survive, it was here they placed their mark on the land. Remnants of tanks storing the water in large cylindrical tubes are still propped up on platforms next to abandoned buildings, and in the jarring heat, hot lashing winds, and des-ert's sparseness, nature took its course. When I first started writing at the Yellowstone residencies, I'd often say: "I am now going down deep into the well."

And these words, in some thirty-eight essays, have sur-vived with their own similar tenacity, belief challenged by self-doubt while on that floodlit night years ago, they were ushered in by a cathartic Scorpio full moon announcing itself over the pinnacles of the mountains.

Questions for Discussion

Prologue: "The Lincoln Memorial"
"Do you remember as a child having a larger than life realization about its meaning that you recognized at a later age?"

Introduction
"At the eleven clock hour at night, have you at times wondered about the meaning of your life? And then come up with realizations?"

Essay 1: "The First Vision"
"When has a natural occurrence, like a blue moon month, signaled important revelations for you?"

Essay 2: "My Imagination"
"Do you remember a particularly satisfying moment or moments using your imagination as a child?"

Essay 3: "French Toast"
"Did you taste a certain food that brought back memories giving you insight into an earlier experience or experiences in your life?"

Essay 4: "The Feminine Mystique"

"Have you ever heard the words of a charismatic leader that inspired you at an young age and gave you direction?"

Essay 6: "The Pilgrimage Home"

"Do you remember the beginning moment that signified a life transforming event later in life?"

Essay 8: "The Artists' Cooperative Comes to Connecticut"

"Do you remember the beginning moment that signified a series of events that would transform your life in later years?"

Essay 9: "Shade Grown Tobacco"

"Has there ever been a time in your life when after an expert told you you would be successful if you tried anything, you took that advice and did succeed in a special way?"

Essay 10: "Contact with an Ancient Stone in England"

"Have you ever had a larger than life experience with an ancient part of nature that was beckoning you and would have much further ramifications in your years to come?"

Essay 11: "Ariadne's Thread"

"Do you remember walking right past a life-changing signal that then repeated itself again and again until you took notice and recognized its significance?"

Essay 12: "Lost in the Sierras"

"Once when you were lost or in danger in nature, do you remember being saved by a special signal or voice that brought you to safety? Did it make you trust life even more?"

Essay 13: "Teddy Roosevelt's Cabin, Yellowstone National Park"

"After working hard for a goal over time that looked like it wouldn't ever succeed, do you remember synchronous events that led you to its success anyway?"

Essay 15: "The Praying Mantis"

"Has an animal or insect totem ever visited you and/or a member of your family during a momentous event in life?"

Essay 16: "Dad's Funeral"

"Have you ever received a special message of clarity from a loved one in the midst of loss or grief?"

Essay 17: "In Search of the Norwegian Lutheran Church"

"Faced with finding a needle in a haystack, with odds stacked completely against it, how did you feel when you actually found it?"

Essay 18: "Avebury: The Awakening"

"How have you felt when an answer to a life-long question mysteriously appeared and an unforgettable event inspired you to this awareness?"

Essay 19: "The Voice that Led Me On"

"Was there a time when you heard to do something or go somewhere that was not expected, and it worked out for the best that you did?"

Essay 20: "Forgiveness is About Letting Go of All Hope for a Better Past"

"How have you learned a new understanding for Forgiveness?"

Essay 21: "Souls Come to Wayfarer's Chapel"

"When a surprising seemingly supernatural encounter occurred unexpectedly, how did you finally come to understand it?"

Essay 22: "The Call from the Blue Nile"

"Did you ever have someone unexpectedly tell you good fortune was on its way to you? How did it work out for you in the end?"

Essay 23: "Swept Away on a Red Carpet"

"When realizing that a new path was surprisingly emerging for you to take at an important juncture in your life, how did it work out for you?"

Essay 24: "The St. Francis Dream"

"Have you ever had a very significant dream that made you trust in faith even more?"

Essay 25: "White Pods and the Battleship Arizona"

"When an historic or meaningful event happened near where you lived, did you understand it differently in a more precious way years later?"

Essay 26: "The Colors of India"

"How did visiting or being in a foreign culture for some time impact you?"

Essay 27: "The Man with the String"

"What experience did you have in a different culture from one you'd grown up in that has resonated with you throughout the years. Why?"

Essay 28: "The Last Day in India"

"What remembrances do you have of the last day in a foreign or different culture you were used to? How do they impact you now?"

Essay 29: "Fair LA, My Family's Final Voyage"

"What do you remember is most special about your family of origin now? How might it also relate to a spirit of place?"

Essay 30: " The Sound of Paper"

"Weathering a major move in your life, what did you finally learn that was useful to you?"

Essay 31: "Tires at Royal Pines, My First Brush with California Fires"

"In a potentially dangerous fire or similar cataclysmic condition, what did you learn about your own coping skills and resourcefulness?"

Essay 32: "There are Many Different Roads to the Oasis in Twenty-Nine Palms"

"Do you have a special place in your life that you can appreciate by approaching it from different vantage points?"

Essay 33: "The Green Dream"

"Have you ever had a significant dream that helped you find a solution to a challenging problem? What did you do?"

Essay 34: "Perseid Meteor Showers and Scorpions"

"Have you ever had a special connection to a small being you came across unexpectedly in a dramatic moment of nature that continues to be a prized understanding of how all beings on this planet are connected?"

Essay 35: "My Grandmother's Gift"

"How do we still receive Gifts of Faith and Strength from our forebears even now?"

Essay 36: "My Sojourn at the Hospital"

"When have you received the message that "You Are Enough" and "Always Have Been?"

Essay 37: "Tsunami Warnings in LA?"

"What personal tsunamis have you been in that have impacted your life, and what did you learn from them?"

Essay 38: "Wonder Valley Writes
The Full Moon in Scorpio"

"Have you had a special experience with a Full Moon that impacted your life course in a new way?"

Acknowledgements

It's the Women's Gatherings in Circles at retreats, workshops and classes for three decades that has fed the writing of "Leap: From Faith to Empowerment." To all of you who participated in these "writing faster than you can think" experiences I've led to discover your unique voice and articulate it, thank you for the shared support and encouragement. I can't personally thank all of you here, so please know I will always be grateful to you.

Thanks to Carla Mann for transforming the manuscript early into its professional form and to David Rasch who worked steadily with me to prepare it for proposals to publishers; also to Holly Parsons who helped coordinate its final steps for proofreading and for all her ongoing support.

Thanks again to David Rasch for envisioning the cover that most accurately expressed the book's metaphysical intent and for being a special presence in my life. And I appreciated so much the astuteness of Regina O'Melveny and Sharon Mosier, writing partners who, week after week during the Covid Pandemic, focused on our writing while the world quaked around us. It was here I believe the words for "Leap" were edited to make them finally worthy for publication. And thank you, Regina, long-term wisdom woman friend, for continuing on as a writing partner, poetry coach, and voice of character and vision to the present.

There is a saying that "Friends are like Stars, you may not be able to always see them, but you know they are there." And I am blessed to have had so many supporters and well-wishers in my life all around the world. I'd like to especially thank Bronwyn Jones, an ever-present stellar supporter and ally from the late 1980's as her husband David Heimenz has also been; and to Denise Helton, dear friend who has also supported my writing especially at UCLA and at other pivotal moments; Christine Eagon, delightful travelling companion through life who introduced me to Glastonbury, UK, and shared Avebury Stone Circle with me; Valerie Silverio, her cousin Linda McKay, Carolyn Barford, another soul sister at Casa del Sol and Ghost Ranch and other luminous places in New Mexico and the Great Sand Dunes of Colorado. Also contributions from, Nancy Laura Joseph, Denise Diamond, Donna Allen, Denise McGregor, Nancy Johnson and her husband Marcelo Carillo, Cyndy Lippert, Janice Lamont, Deanne Larsen, Mary Lumsden, Louise Zawadski, Bob and Isolde Lata, Alicia Rowe, Lynn Heinz, Mary Ann Wilson, Susan Hecht, Diane Dorman, Paula Hollie, Suzanne Grant, Maty Konigsberg, Cynthia Shepard, Valerie McKean, Phyllis Johnson, Char Sieg, Mariana Camalleri, Virginia Crowder, Maggie Rae Abbot, Anne Franklin, Tanya Chakraborty, Cynthia Riola, Les Gin, Fu-Ding Cheng, Regina Jones, Lance Johnson and Jane Gnoza,

Stefanie, Charles and Ava Howard, and favorite supporters Phillip and Roberta Gold, Jocelyn Brimo in my recent classes have meant so much to me.

And thanks to Sandra Richards, past Director, UCR, University of California, Riverside Extension of the OLLI Program there, and Johnna Norris, at its Palm Desert and Mary Ann Wilson at its UCLA counterparts for the classes I've taught there and their support. One last shout-out goes to supporters at the Meher Baba Retreat Center in Myrtle Beach, South Carolina, especially to Jackie Boyce, who helped to organize wonderful workshops there. Love always to the Connecticut clan: Katharine King, Regina Mocey-Hanton & Steve Hanton, Peter Skolem, Kitty Winslow, Maureen and Dick Liebler, Shelley and Jessie Smith.

A special salute goes to favorite Idyllwildians, with whom I've been fortunate to share their special community, especially at Spirit Mountain Retreat; to Mary Morse, Director, who I've shared special times with developing retreats and workshops, and our forays on the "Celebration of the Circle" sacred site tours. To Carol McClintic, Barb Reese, Suzie Bennett, Charlene Chindlund, Hollis Fulmor, Micki Aybar, Elaine Gantman, Sheila Kloss, Cathy Mauge, Esther Kennedy, among many others. My hat is off to Marilyn O'Connor who convinced me that starry night in Joshua Tree 13 years ago to start writing "Leap," and to Marilyn Sequoia, another Pisces ally, first met in Yellowstone National Park, who created the calligraphic art work, "Katya Leads By Going." Thanks to her husband Jeffrey Laird for his assistance as well.

The Sisterhood extends far and wide, and especially to Glastonbury, UK, home of the Sophia's Writing Group started there, with special love to Patricia and John Caswell, Ingelise Jensen, Seppie Hope, Carole Fox, Valerie Smith, Maggie Stewart, Felicia Chang, Lorye Keats Hopper, Elizabeth Keller, Stacey Camfield and Gabrielle and especially to Sabrina Dearborn who wrote the preface to "Bringing the Soul Back Home: Writing in the New Consciousness" (published by "Compass Books", UK in 2009). Phillipe Ullens and wife Dominque, owners of the prized Henge Shop inside the Avebury Stone Circle in the UK, Nicholas Mann and Pippa Glasson, Bernard Chandler, designer of "Awakening in Avebury: A Woman's Call to Pilgrimage," (published in the UK 2017), John Flanagan and wife Meredith Flanagan, Dilys Guilford, and so many others have made this a lasting place of the heart.

This book would not exist except for the outstanding crew at the Blue Jay Ink in Ojai, California. Thank you so much Dave Reeser and Emma Kienzle for your patience especially during my knee replacement this year and for your astute capability during this time we've worked together to make "Leap" become a reality!! Other authors from Antioch University's Master's Degree program (Los Angeles) have appreciated your aptitude as well, and I'm glad I am now part of this group.

And lastly love to those of my family of origin, my sister Linda/Lolani, a bright light in my life, brothers Marc and David, nephews Josh, Jon, and Ben, niece Jenny and great niece Tiana. Cousin Harry McKell from Gargrave, UK continues to be an special link to my family history there. Thank you. You are the circle around which the larger sacred world circles exist of chosen family and friends.

I am blessed to have had you in my life.
Thank you, one and all! Katya

Photo: Bronwyn Jones. Cornwall. U.K.

About the Author

Katya was awarded her MFA in Creative Writing from Antioch University, Los Angeles, a summa cum laude BA degree from the University of Connecticut in Organizational Management and creative writing, and a Certificate in Museum Studies from the graduate Museum Studies program at the University of Southern California. Her writer was born in Paris, France at the age of ten, and she has published books and poetry in both England and the United States. She started the "Celebration of the Circle" sacred site writing tours for women in 2000 to bring them to a deeper connection with the Divine Feminine in England, Ireland, Hawaii, Yellowstone National Park, and New Mexico. She has led weekend writing retreats at Spirit Mountain Retreat for 30f years where she is currently its writer-in-residence, and began "Ten Thousand Waves of Women's Voices," in 2017, an organization that supports all women in the world to discover and claim their authentic voice. Her poetry now focuses on the Oneness that humanity is moving towards, often through the appreciation of the spirit of nature.

*Quote on Introduction by Johann Wolfgang von Goethe